Media Money Myths:

A Personal and Professional Journey of Debunking

Dr. Mark Harmon, Professor of Journalism and Electronic Media, University of Tennessee, Knoxville.

I0455154

Chapters

Tables

End Notes

Prologue

Sometime around 1971 or 1972, when I was a teenager strolling through the storefront office of some long-abandoned political cause, I picked up a copy of *America, Inc.: who owns and operates the United States*, a blunt and well-documented book by *Washington Post* reporters Morton Mintz and Jerry Cohen.[1] The thesis was devastating—a growing corporate world was concentrating and manipulating markets, corrupting politics, and thwarting regulation and all other checks on abuses.

Despite, or perhaps because of, the upheavals of Vietnam and the civil rights movement (and later Watergate), it was a time of comparatively high regard for our institutions. It was a time of faith in self-governance. We may not have, or ever achieve, a perfect union, but we knew the direction to travel. Every year we should safeguard and expand the liberties of our people. We should expand educational and economic opportunities for the next generation. We should set standards for safe products, good wages, and a clean environment. Peace and justice weren't slogans, but goals. We may have disagreed on speed or the proper mix of public and private action, but "we the people" made sense and held power.

Now it all seems so quaint, naïve, and distant—a foggy memory or some rose-colored nostalgia. Yet, the descriptive data and historical records are there, like some dusty LP vinyl record just waiting for someone to remember how to start the turntable and nestle the needle into the groove.

I have reached an age in life when I can remember and characterize decades. Once you've passed a half-century on this planet the years seem to rush by in a cruel trick of perspective. When you are 50, a year is one-fiftieth of your life, a bullet train zooming past. When you are six, a year is one-sixth of your life; it seems like an eternity, especially as your fresh, young mind daily interacts with new discoveries.

So this book must not, is not, cannot be a grouchy reminiscence of how great things were, and how crappy they are now. The fresh young mind encountering these words deserves better than that. Instead, it is a call to action, a recognition that

some of trends and messages we take for granted today are not
moral, or reasonable, or sustainable, or inevitable. Where we are
as a community is a result of human choices, good and bad.
Further, with good choices—drawn not only from recent
experience but also the good ideas of multiple generations and
the even better ideas of people still to come—we can chart an
inspiring path. We can answer the question raised by Elvis
Costello, "What's so funny about peace, love, and
understanding?" And the firm reply is "Nothing. Nothing at all.
Let's get to work."

Many other books may be viewed as inspirations to this
one. Edward Jay Epstein's *News from Nowhere* took a critical
look at structural-functional factors molding the processes and
outcomes of network TV news. Mintz and Cohen came out with
a good sequel, *Power, Inc.* Ben Bagdikian published the first of
several editions regarding *Media Monopoly.* Howard Zinn wrote
the exceptionally valuable *A People's History of the United States*,
re-establishing the progressive struggle against plutocracy as a
motivating factor in the story of our lives. In the United

Kingdom, the Glasgow University Media Group began producing insightful critiques of that status-quo lean of the BBC.[2]

That list should give a clue to the path I have taken, and the touchstones to my approach. I was the nerdy kid in high school and college who was on the debate team, wrote columns for the student paper, and took to the airwaves to deliver radio news. I am by training and inclination a journalist, one who has spent the bulk of his career in the classroom as a teacher. I've always cared deeply about public policy, and even ran for Congress, and later was elected to my county commission.[3] Others have traveled different paths (sociology, education, technology, economics, public service, the creative arts) but likely will arrive at roughly the same place, the grim realization that we are in an era of growing oligopoly and plutocracy. Tragically, we rarely tell that story. Thus, we have the need for a book about our mediated money myths.

Chapter One reviews some important and disturbing recent developments in American wealth. Likely the most significant change, declining economic mobility, is the topic of

Chapter Two. Chapter Three debunks an all-too-common myth, demonstrating how mass media tend to drift not toward the liberal, but toward conservative and corporate perspectives.

Chapter Four shows how the reasons we give why others are poor or wealthy are a defining rift on our politics, one seemingly immune to challenging information and reporting. As noted in Chapter Five, the central message of television (indeed, most media) is not violence, but commercial consumption— imperatives to buy stuff. Chapter Six brings all these debunking exercises into Election 2012; and Chapter Seven pulls all the threads together into a call for action.

I also need to say a few words about approach and writing style. In my career I've written copy for outlets as diverse as television newscasts, newspaper columns, books, magazines, radio reports, and academic journals. This book is written in what I hope will be a popular and direct style. It does, however, draw from academic research. So, to avoid disrupting the reader, that supporting material is presented at the close as endnotes, appendices, and tables.

Chapter 1. A Duke Costs More to Keep Up than a Dreadnought

The numbers are startling, almost overwhelming. The six children of Walmart's founders have the same net worth as the bottom 41.5 percent of all American earners. The richest 400 Americans control as much wealth as the bottom half of American earners. The top ten percent of U. S. households control 74.5 percent of the country's wealth. The top one percent in the U.S. between 1979 and 2007 had income growth of 275 percent, compared to just 18 percent for the bottom fifth of our earners, and an actual income decline during that time frame for the very poor.[4]

In the modest economic recovery of 2009 to 2010, the top one percent of income earners in the U. S. captured 93 percent of income growth. Nobel Prize-winning economist Joseph Stiglitz had other bad news:

> It would be one thing if the high incomes of those at the top were the result of greater contributions to society, but the Great Recession showed otherwise; even bankers who had led the

global economy, as well as their own firms, to the brink of ruin, received outsized bonuses.

A closer look at those at the top reveals a disproportionate role for rent-seeking: some have obtained their wealth by exercising monopoly power; others are CEOs who have taken advantage of deficiencies in corporate governance to extract for themselves an excessive share of corporate earnings; and still others have use political connections to benefit from government munificence—either excessively high prices for what the government buys (drugs), or excessively low prices for what the government sells (mineral rights).

Likewise, part of the wealth of those in finance comes from exploiting the poor, through predatory lending and abusive credit-card practices. Those at the top, in such cases, are enriched at the direct expense of those at the bottom.[5]

The chance to achieve that upper-income rung also is in decline. Social mobility is sometimes a difficult thing to pin down, but the Organization for Economic Cooperation and Development crunched the numbers on 34 countries and found U.S. intergenerational mobility low and declining. Contrary to popular Horatio Alger mythology, we have now slipped behind every developed country studied except possibly Italy and the United Kingdom.[6]

Education often is touted as a means to achieve social mobility.[7] Recent numbers, however, suggest that road hardly is a meritocracy. The U.S. Department of Education in 1988 began a study of students then in 8th grade, following them for 12 years. A notable pattern could be found in the data about college graduation. Those who in 1988 were in the lowest quartile of family income but the top quartile of math test scores had a 29 percent college graduation rate. The inverse, top quartile of family income but bottom quartile of math scores, had a 30 percent college graduation rate.[8]

America's wealthy also enjoy a special advantage in legacy admissions to elite colleges. One recent study at Duke found that persons admitted because of a parent's legacy status, compared to their non-legacy counterparts, were more likely to be white, Protestant, and have attended private schools. Family income was substantially higher, even compared to non-legacies whose parents had attended college. The legacy students also performed worse academically than non-legacies in their first semester or two, but caught up.[9]

We've seen these factors before—huge gaps between rich and poor, low social mobility, and a political and economic deck stacked by the wealthy and powerful. One must add to the mix compliant news media that distract, divide, and repeat mythologies rather point to abuses. The situation becomes exacerbated when the pampered second and third generations of the elite get into jobs that make money by moving money, using ever more complicated financial schemes that use other people's money in risky maneuvers. The initial gains are maximized and privatized, but the inevitable losses are socialized. It happened during the stock market trigger to the Great Depression, the Savings and Loan debacles of the 1980s, and the Wall Street collapse fueled by and occurring at the close of the George Walker Bush administration. Bush the Lesser is himself a third-generation child of privilege, one doomed to some measure of success despite himself, and leaving behind for others a sociopathic collection of wreckage to nearly every institution that every was good to him—notably the National Guard, the Supreme Court, and the Republican Party.

We run the risk of creating a permanent upper class, transmitting its poor morals (greed that grows into avarice, sloth in some propped-up ne'er do wells, and pride in assuming and asserting morality superiority over those who are poor) from one generation to the next. We simply cannot sustain the economic, political, and environmental cost of such an entitlement culture. We first, however, must disabuse ourselves of the current misuse of the term entitlement. The term should not be used for systems that working people have paid into for years—unemployment insurance, Medicare, and Social Security.

The yearly numbers on those programs are large, but pale in comparison to the entitlements assumed by the super rich. Initially, the super rich assume and that their major source of income, capital gains, is more valuable than the wage and salary income earned by the sweat and smarts of everyone else. Thus, capital gains are taxed at a theoretical maximum of 15% while wage and salary income is taxed at a much higher rate. Secondly, these theoretical maximums are not met because the very wealthy now rent politicians as needed, largely for the purposes of creating tax loopholes and converting a progressive tax structure into a regressive one.

Finally, corporations, legal fictions now treated under law as persons and disproportionately controlled by the super rich, assume the right to use huge chunks of public resources with little regard for equity or effect. Courts protect their wealth from and resources from crime, but the white-collar crimes of Wall Street largely go unprosecuted. The most egregious cases sometimes yield a settlement, often for less money that that stolen and with no jail time for executives or even an admission of fault.

The resources of the wealthy are protected by an immense military, but it will be the sons and daughters of the struggling working class who will do the fighting and dying in wars—wars made more likely by a political drift away from congressional, shared sacrifice, and public opinion checks on using the military unwisely.[10] The super wealthy and their corporate extensions also assume the right to use our public roads, bridges, power grid, and other infrastructure (not to mention benefitting from the increased skills and research developments of our education infrastructure) while constantly seeking new ways to shift the cost of it to everyone else.

The corporate/wealthy nexus of power also assumes the right to foul our land, air, and water with little to no responsibility for the long-term health consequences. Now lobbyists for the corporate/wealthy combo pack are seeking to roll back what minimal standards we've achieved (after decades of struggle) for workplace safety, decent pay and benefits, and pollution restriction.

The super wealthy exist in multiple states of denial, just as many exist in multiple states of residence—and not just for tax purposes. Not many of the rest of us use the word summer as a verb. Tucked away in gated neighborhoods and exclusive clubs, it's easy for the super rich to associate only with their own kind. Eventually some even may internalize the propaganda spun for the saps relying on talk radio and Fox News. The one percent may think of themselves as "job creators," even those like Mitt Romney who mostly toiled as asset strippers and job exporters.

Labor Department figures are that the vast majority, at least nine out of every ten of us, primarily earn our income by working for someone else. When we look in the mirror each morning, we are looking at a job creator. Our consumer spending fuels the economy. Our improved productivity could go into a healthy mix of better pay, more benefits, training, workplace improvements in our tools, maybe even employee stock ownership plans. Sadly, our stagnant wages and closing factories are testament to the distant, detached short-term profit artists. It is no surprise then that CEO pay has jumped from 42 times average blue-collar worker pay in 1980 to 380 times median worker pay in 2011. Executives nowhere else on Earth have anything close to that rate of compensation.[11]

Just as earlier we had to rescue the word entitlement from misuse, here we must salvage populism. A certain faux populism has been generated by radical right flacks, attempts to redirect working-class anger against the poor, not the rich;

against the government, not the corporate power brokers.

Immigrants, foreigners, and the few remaining places to get

some progressive messages also get twisted into targets. The

Occupy Movement represents a fresh effort to dismiss the faux

populism for the real thing—sincere outrage at more than 30

years of disingenuous public policy and greedy economic choices

that have devastated the middle class for the further enrichment

of the incredibly wealthy.

Of course, such a notion is outside the traditional and

acceptable news frames of persons who professionally evolved

in corporate media systems. The multifaceted angles and

grassroots organization mean that each protester brings an

individual set of emphases about the larger problem. Further, it

seems anytime your broad message contains the word

corporation, many confused news organizations caricaturize you

as an inchoate grab bag of causes.

That's a shame. Since California's 1978's Proposition 13

we've seen a U. S. counterrevolution of the rich. It has created an

extreme state of affairs that not environmentally, politically, or economically sustainable. So we need to get past our fascination with winning the lottery, and dismiss our fantasy that a mystery relative will leave us millions. Also, we may want to put aside for later reflection thoughts that a mysterious religious phenomenon will make planning unnecessary. We need to rekindle a time-proven American notion, planning for better systems and outcomes for future generations. Here is my starter list of principles, policies, and goals to get us headed in the proper direction.

First and foremost, by whatever means necessary (constitutional amendment, new appointments to the Supreme Court), we must overturn two very bad Supreme Court decisions. Buckley v. Valeo (1976) declared giving money the functional equivalent of speech. Citizens United v. FEC (2010), in the name of that "speech," set up corporations and any other groups to buy elections or scare off candidates with unlimited, unaccountable donations. Both decisions must go for all other steps to work. Further, other states should adopt the campaign public finance plans first established by Maine, but with later variations in Vermont, Massachusetts, and Arizona. Iowa's non-partisan method of redistricting also deserves emulation.

The Antitrust Division of the Justice Department, the Securities and Exchange Commission, and the new Consumer Financial Protection Bureau need to be more than paper tigers. Let's appoint aggressive leaders, quintuple their enforcement budget, and get to work on crime in the suites.

Then we can reverse the trend, now exceeding 30 years, of shifting the total tax burden from the wealthy and corporations to the middle and working classes. Tax capital gains at the same rate as wage and salary income. End the Bush-era tax breaks for annual income in excess of a quarter-million dollars. The added revenues then can be used for badly needed and job-creating work: repairing our bridges and roads, creating a more efficient energy grid that incorporates many more solar and wind projects, developing a high-speed rail network, improving public school resources, and tripling the amount of money available for college grants. We also should increase the amount of loan forgiveness and speed the timetable of that forgiveness for teaching, Peace Corps or AmeriCorps VISTA service.

The U. S. now spends more on our military than the next fourteen nations combined, including many allies.[12] Careful audits, reduced reliance on no-bid contracts, and elimination of unneeded programs must proceed, saving billions needed for both other programs and deficit/debt reduction.

Most of us never see the annual paycheck "cap out" where we stop being taxed for Social Security at $106,800. End the "cap out" to help assure the future strength of the program. We also can put the proven low overhead of Medicare to use, creating a "buy into Medicare" option for all. Of course, we also should create a foreclosure moratorium until our homeowners recover from Wall Street abusing their mortgages as casino chips. A sane system of mortgage lending can return only after: those who abused the system and broke the law are convicted, new bank regulations are in place and enforced, banks resume lending and stop sitting on a mountain of cash, and homeowners show signs of recovery.

In the United States few things are as lopsidedly distributed as wealth, certainly not intelligence, talent, skill, persistence, creativity, initiative, and enthusiasm. A return to a thriving middle class with the social mobility to match their aspirations is a moral, political, and economic imperative. It will improve so many aspects of out lives and our communities, and even promote a type of prosperity that benefits even the already wealthy, initial howls of protest and name calling notwithstanding.

The current stacked deck works for too few and stifles the abilities of too many. As a rule, we are born individually, die individually, and our rights are guaranteed individually, and quite properly so. Yet, our lives are made better when we care about one another. We took a seriously wrong turn decades ago when we let candidate Ronald Reagan get away with the question, "Are you better off today than you were four years ago?" The error was compounded when he asserted government was the problem not the solution.

Our response should have been, "What a selfish question! The questions should be: Are we better off as a community? Are our air and water cleaner? Do our kids have stronger opportunities for learning? Do we use the tools of government against the excesses of corporate power or do we put those tools in their hands?"

We are better guided by a different presidential quote. John F. Kennedy warned us, "If a free society cannot help the many who are poor, it cannot save the few who are rich." As a national community we cannot afford to maintain the current high concentration of wealth. More than a century ago Britain's David Lloyd George lamented, "A fully equipped Duke costs as much to keep up as two Dreadnoughts...is just as great a terror and lasts longer."[13] The only modern updates needed are to substitute carrier groups for dreadnoughts and billionaires for Dukes. The super-wealthy are getting too expensive to maintain, and this unnatural state is maintained largely by poor public policy choices.

Finally, as the public policy is set aright, let us recall the very important personal choices that also can help us retain a socially and economically mobile nation with a thriving middle class. We must use our consumer dollars wisely, avoiding companies that fail to maintain high moral standards. Even as we set right current political and economic stagnation, we must reject cost-benefit analysis as the only measure of our choices. It is a shallow mind that thinks it can put a price tag on a beautiful sunset, and an even shallower one that sets its default value at zero. We must read to children, involve them in discussions, and get them thinking critically about the world around them. We must avoid shallow materialism; and we must model to kids our love for them, as well as our loves for beauty and truth.

Chapter 2. Horatio Alger is Dead (and I'm not feeling that well myself)

Rags-to-riches stories are woven into the narrative of American greatness. Pulling one's self up by one's own bootstraps often is the phrase used both to encourage and to exalt this phenomenon. The rags-to-riches theme was so common in the popular stories by Horatio Alger, Jr., that the author's name itself is now shorthand for the theme.

Malcolm Forbes wrote a quick summary of Horatio Alger's literary life that can be a good starting point for a review of the significance of his work, and how modern usages of his name often are at odds with his actual themes and messages:

"Horatio Alger wrote so many rags-to-riches novels that his name became synonymous with going from poverty to great pelf...Alger's characters always ended up triumphant, happy, and rich. He wrote more than 100 happy endings, to tales such as *Dan the newsboy*, *Ben the luggage boy*, *Phil the fiddler*, and *Paul the peddler*. There were *Andy Grant's pluck* and *Joe's luck*. Most famous of all was one of his earliest stories, *Ragged Dick*. At least an entire generation of boys learned that virtue and hard work always were rewarded by wealth and honor.

"Alger stuck by his poor-boy-makes good formula, often basing his stories on youths he met in post-Civil War New York City at the Newsboys' Lodging House. He churned out books in just a few weeks, earning him an estimated $20,000 a year, an incredible sum for a century ago."[14]

An impressive list of persons claim to have been influenced by Alger's work to try harder and to aspire to greatness. Former New York Governor and presidential candidate Al Smith was a newsboy on Manhattan's Lower East Side when he spent spare dimes on Alger books. Poet Carl Sandburg sought the books from the public library, as did the boy who became Francis Cardinal Spellman, Archbishop of New York. Ohio Governor Michael V. DiSalle credits Alger's themes as an important influence. Other Alger readers included: former Postmaster General and Coca-Cola executive James A. Farley, Benjamin Fairless of U. S. Steel; future U. S. presidents Gerald Ford and Ronald Reagan; writers Joyce Kilmer, Ernest Hemingway, F. Scott Fitzgerald, Theodore Dreiser, Jack London, Richard Wright, and Upton Sinclair; sports figures Christy

Mathewson of the New York Giants and Knute Rockne of Notre Dame.[15]

Publishing records from the time are frustratingly incomplete and inexact. The most conservative estimates put the tally at 15 million books sold, but several researchers and biographers put the total at more like 100 to 500 million from all publishers in all versions, especially the ten-cent clothbound variety, not to mention periodical sales of magazines that carried his serials.[16]

Frank Gruber tallied that, "Alger published no more than six million words in a career that spanned over thirty years. He wrote 109 works, averaging 50,000 words each and possibly another hundred thousand words of short material. He averaged only 150,000 words a year for his writing lifetime. I have known writers who wrote that much in a month." Gruber, writing in 1961, noted that more copies have sold of Alger's work than any author who ever lived.[17]

At one time or another more than 60 publishers had put out at least one Alger book. Alger's works were so popular that

even the author's death in 1899 did not stop the phenomenon.
Edward Stratemeyer, an editor and himself a prolific writer of
boys' books, was a friend of Alger who most likely cobbled
together his own ideas with some notes left behind by Alger to
craft another eleven books.[18]

Literary critics and literary historians rarely mention
Alger.[19] Those who have done so often were blunt and negative
about Alger's immensely popular works.

"The moral tales of the nineteenth century were being
replaced be stories nearer to reality," wrote John Tebbel. "The
reaction started in schools and libraries, institutions which had
long regarded Alger with suspicion as a subverter of taste in the
young. Teachers now openly condemned his books, and they
were removed from the shelves of both school and public
libraries. As early as August, 1907, the Worcester public library
board ruled that no Alger book could be circulated from its
shelves, and this action was widely imitated in various parts of
the country. Paradoxically, the more Alger was roundly

condemned by educators and librarians, the more his posthumous sales increased."[20]

He may have been significant at the start of the 20th century, but by 1947 a poll taken in seven New York Boys and Girls Clubs found that 92% of the children had never heard of him, and only one percent had read any of his books.[21] Three-quarters of the way through the 20th century he was being dismissed critically as irrelevant, dead as a Dodo.[22]

Biographer Carol Nackenoff makes the case that Alger really was a "genteel moralist," presenting "moral guidance through fiction in a way that has eluded supporters and critics alike." She argues that the "interests, values, and themes articulated in Alger's prize-winning essays at Harvard pervade his literary career." Alger, indeed, followed his father's footsteps in attending Harvard and attending divinity school. A student of classics, Alger advanced ideas of Harvard neo-Platonists and Unitarian moralists such as Harvard President Edward Everett and Unitarian Minister William Ellery Channing. Alger did not enjoy the wealth of his Boston Brahmin classmates. In fact, he needed financial aid to complete his studies. He had been born in Chelsea, now Revere, in 1832. Financial difficulties for his father forced a family move to Marlborough, then a rural village on the outskirts of Boston.[23]

Alger's brief career after Harvard as a young Unitarian minister is the source of lingering controversy among Alger biographers. In late 1864 Horatio Alger, Jr., accepted an appointment to minister to the First Unitarian Church and Society in Brewster, Massachusetts. He still sought, and sometimes succeeded, in publishing poems and stories in various publications. Within 15 months Alger had fled Brewster. Rumors of the molestation of young boys prompted his hasty exit. Alger never confirmed or denied the claim, but spoke to being "imprudent." The church committee dealt with the matter by not rehiring Alger. Parents threatened charges but none were filed. Instead the committee wrote a blistering note to the American Unitarian Association in Boston.[24]

One biographer cast some doubt on the severity and specifics of the events in Brewster, but it is clear that Alger in his words, deeds, and at least one poem--Friar Anselmo's Sin--

recognized in himself a need for redemption and to make

amends.[25] No similar scandal was noted in the remainder of

Alger's life; he then devoted that life to writing moral tales in

which the heroes are young boys, and in his public life did not

use the term reverend in reference to himself.[26]

The biographical record is clear that Horatio Alger, Jr.,

likely would be surprised by some of the persons and

enterprises to which his name and literary themes have been

attached. Biographers Gary Scharnhorst and Jack Bales point out

that Alger was distressed by profiteering, corruption, stock

manipulation, the Standard Oil machinations with leading

railroads. Far from being a capitalist ideologue, Alger was not an

advocate necessarily for wage or price competition. He believed

in a living wage and liked economic cooperatives, and in later

works he even criticized the profit motive.[27] Scharnhorst and

Bales stated:

> "Alger was a mugwump, a liberal
> Republican committed to principles of fair prices

and decent wages, a critic of sharp business
practices and cutthroat competition. He was
neither an apologist for the wealthy class nor a
stalking horse for industrial capitalism. Rather,
his appeal was fundamentally nostalgic. He often
set his tales in idealized villages modeled upon
preindustrial Marlborough. His heroes never
worked in mechanized factories, and in his later
stories they were more often the sons of poor
farmers than indigent street Arabs. Whereas
Alger wrote his early juvenile fiction to publicize
the work of the Catholic Aid Society and kindred
institutions, many of the stories he wrote in the
1880s and 1890s were thinly-disguised critiques
of the corrupt captains of industry."[28]

Terms such as "rags to riches," "Horatio Alger," and

pulling one's self up by one's "own bootstraps" are important to

American self-identity. However, social and economic mobility

in the United States is in trouble. It is less frequent than in past

generations, the U. S. now trails nearly all developed nations in

measures of movement, and one mechanism of mobility,

education, is losing its effectiveness in that regard.

Yet, for the all theme repetition, the actual rate of social

and economic mobility, by almost any measure tracked, has been

declining in the United States for several decades. Thus, U. S.

journalism faces a conundrum. Does it follow society's metanarratives of story telling, the master myths of news as described by Jack Lule in *Daily News, Eternal Stories.*[29] Or, does journalistic content "prick the bubble" of the myth, pointing out its unlikelihood and its declining probability?

The challenge is particularly acute for broadcast news with its traditions of short, simple, visual, and emotional storytelling. Print, web, and broadcast news all can and do employ a compelling case study technique as a way to personalize and to demonstrate an issue. Broadcast news, however, may lack the time or depth to muddy the matter with counter-thematic questions of scale, scope, and trends.

Social Mobility Data: Overwhelming, Consistent, and Largely Ignored

The Organization for Economic Cooperation and Development (OECD) examined established intergenerational mobility measures, such as father-to-son earnings and education, and concluded, "Mobility in earnings, wages and education across generations is relatively low in France, southern European countries, the United Kingdom and the United States. By contrast, such mobility tends to be higher in Australia, Canada and the Nordic countries."[30] The OECD findings echo work by several researchers during the decade of the 2000s.[31]

A Brookings Institution and Pew Charitable Trusts report declared, "All Americans do not have an equal shot at getting ahead, and one's chances are largely dependent on one's parents' economic position...The chances of making it to the top of the income distribution decline steadily as one's parents' family income decreases."[32]

Most research on income mobility divides the population into fourths or fifths. Those who look at intergenerational movement from one-fifth (or quintile) to another find most motion is in the middle of the family income scale. Someone born in the middle (3rd quintile) could move up to the 2nd or down to the 4th. The poor and rich have the highest likelihood of staying in that position across generations.   Further, noted the Brookings/Pew Report, the increasing inequality of income distribution in the U. S. means that "since the rungs of the ladder are further apart than they used to be, the effects of family background on one's ultimate economic success are larger and may persist for a longer period of time."[33] The report also noted that the U. S. falls in the mid-range of international mobility measures, and the lowest mobility rates were clustered at the bottom of the U.S. income ladder. "The findings from cross-country research challenge the traditional view of the United States as a land with more mobility and opportunity than other countries," concluded the report.[34]

While bottom quintile to top quintile hopping is highly unlikely in a generation, storied and extreme rags-to-riches stories are even more rare. Tom Hertz at the Center for American Progress found that children from low-income families have only a one percent chance of reaching the top five percent of income distribution. Children in the middle quintile did not fare much better, just a 1.8 percent likelihood of reaching that same high-income group. By contrast, the children of the upper strata had a 22 percent rate of reaching the top five percent of income.[35]

Hertz further found that the U.S. trailed France, Germany, Sweden, Canada, Finland, Norway, and Denmark in intergenerational mobility. Only the United Kingdom had less class mobility than the United States among similar high-income countries. The "rungs farther apart" phenomenon also has been growing worse. The Brookings/Pew report points out there has been no income advancement, adjusted for inflation, for the younger generations. In fact, men in their thirties as a group have on average 12 percent less income than their fathers' generation at the same age. The authors concluded that the "up-escalator" that has historically endured so each generation would do better than the last may not be working very well.[36]

Michael Moore penned a devastating critique of the Horatio Alger myth as a key factor regarding ineffective public action against CEO abuses. He wrote:

> It is first prescribed to us as children in the form of a fairy tale—but a fairy tale that can actually come true! It is the Horatio Alger myth. Alger was one of the most popular American

writers of the late 1800s. His stories featured characters from impoverished backgrounds who, through pluck and determination and hard work, were able to make huge successes of themselves in this land of boundless opportunity. The message was that anyone can make it in America, and make it big.

We are addicted to this happy rags-to-riches myth in this country…. Despite all the damage and all the evidence to the contrary, the average American still wants to hand on to this belief that maybe, just maybe, he or she (mostly he) just might make it big after all. So don't attack the rich man, because one day that rich man may be me![37]

The Horatio Alger/Own Bootstraps/Rags to Riches Myth certainly has a strong presence in public opinion. A Pew poll in 2009 asked respondents to rate on a zero-to-ten scale about how well statements described the American Dream. "Being able to succeed regardless of the economic circumstances in which you were born" scored a perfect ten with 34% of respondents, and another 26% giving it an eight or nine. Similarly, the statement "your children being better off financially than you" scored ten with 35% of respondents, and eight or nine with another 29%.[38]

CBS News / *New York Times* several times has asked poll respondents, "Do you think it's still possible to start out poor in this country, work hard, and become rich?" The numbers have jumped around a bit, but show a consistent and strong majority for the possibility.

Date	Poss.	Not	Don't Know	Sample Size
April 22-26, 1981*	67	28	3	1439
January 16-19, 1983	57	38	5	1597
July 31-August 3, 1988 **	59	35	6	1353
February 22-24, 1996	70	27	3	1223
March 20-21, 1996	78	18	4	1001
April 15-20, 1998 (NYT)	70	29	2	1395
February 6-10, 2000	84	13	3	1499
July 13, 2003 (Hispanic oversample)	70	27	3	3092
June 26-28, 2007	81	18	1	836
April 1-5, 2009	72	24	4	998

* Alternate wording: Do you think it's possible nowadays for someone in this country to start out poor, and become rich by working hard? Two percent volunteered it was possible through other means.
** Alternate wording: Do you think it's as possible now as it was when you finished school to start out poor in this country, work hard, and become rich?[39]

Of course, as authors Stephen McNamee and Robert Miller have pointed out in *The Meritocracy Myth*, "the mere *possibility* of getting rich is not the same as the *likelihood* of getting rich." They further remind us that meritorious personal characteristics such as talent and hard work certainly play a role in social and economic mobility, but these traits themselves have social origins. High moral standards, they note, can work against such mobility. "It is not innate capacity alone, or the proper frame of mind alone that makes a difference. Rather it is a *combination* of opportunity and these factors that make a difference."[40]

Chapter One already has noted how education no longer works well as an engine of social mobility. Allan Ornstein adds that such opportunities overall are shrinking, leaving meritocracy a hollow shell or a false promise:

> A new form of arrogance can develop by the creation of meritocracy, by the same people who once believed in and exemplified the political theories of Jeffersonian democracy and the stories

> of Horatio Alger. If true merit becomes associated
> with *heredity* or innate ability, as it is often
> construed, as opposed to the notion of *opportunity*,
> [then] meritocracy becomes less of a virtue and
> more of a propaganda tool for patricians and
> conservatives to wave and use against the
> populace who have fewer opportunities because of
> their social and economic status.[41]

One really cannot write about class mobility without mentioning the subject of news coverage of class, and television news does not have a good record in this regard. Don Heider and Koji Fuse conducted a combined content analysis and participant observation study of Denver local television news in July 1998. Newscast producers and reporters well understood the desired audience for their program was suburban women aged 25 to 54. Though class rarely was stated, this targeted demographic played a key role in news selection decisions. The poor simply weren't "on the radar" of local television news, and only 1.9 percent of all stories during the study period were about the needy.[42]

Jack Lule's "Master Myths of News" draws inspiration from: Mircea Eliade, a Romanian philosopher and historian of religion, who saw myth as quintessentially human; Joseph

Campbell who found myth ubiquitous; and Carl Jung who saw

myth as essential. Lule readily admits the claim can be

overstated—a house fire story can be just a house fire story—

but he argues that news has habits, traditions, and shortcuts that

all draw from the human traditions of storytelling. After all,

news people do refer to their output as stories, not just reports.

Lule discerns seven master myths in news. One from his

list, The Hero, is quite pervasive and includes elements of

success and social mobility:

> Heroes remind people that they can succeed, that they can achieve greatness. Hercules, Karna, Gilgamesh, Ulysses, Achilles, and Samson are just a few heroes whose exploits are celebrated in myth. Heroes also subtly offer limitations by telling stories of *who* can succeed and *how*. As myth, news stories too regularly celebrate the exploits of heroes. From sports stars to movie stars, astronauts to artists, presidents to prime ministers, the news tells stories of heroic men and women. The news produces and reproduces the timeless pattern: the humble birth, the early mark of greatness, the quest, the triumph, and the return. The news daily brings us stories of the Hero, stories that proclaim—but also help define—greatness.[43]

Do U. S. newscasts tell us such heroic stories, but ignore the reality of declining social mobility? One complicating factor in answering that question is the increasing political polarization of continuous ("24/7") cable news operations. Fox News has a documented and deserved pro-Republican and pro-conservative slant,[44] and conservative viewers seek it out for that reason.[45] MSNBC recently has offered, at least in its prime-time programs, a contrary point of view.

Examining U. S. TV News Coverage

I decided to look into what picture of social and economic mobility U. S. television news programs present. The past observations and research strongly suggest that U. S. television news tilts strongly toward repetition of the mythology rather than any questioning of it. I also took the opportunity to test some political polarization of the topic in two ways. Initially, whether the 24/7 cable news operations Fox News and MSNBC are more likely than stories from the network newscasts (CBS Evening News, NBC Nightly News, and ABC World News) to invoke and involve political parties in the text of social and economic mobility stories. Secondly, I tested whether, as one might suspect, Fox News does the least amount of myth debunking, and MSNBC the most myth debunking.

Fortunately, I had a great tool to use, the broadcast transcripts area of Lexis Nexis Academic. It allowed me to do a keyword search for: economic mobility, social mobility, upward mobility, downward mobility, Horatio Alger, own bootstraps, or rags to riches. The search was conducted on January 6-7, 2011, but covered all available dates for transcripts. The search yielded 55 transcripts from MSNBC, 68 from Fox News, and 46 from the network TV evening newscasts, ABC World News, CBS Evening News, and NBC Nightly News. By far, the greatest number of "hits" was for rags to riches at 84, compared to 41 for upward mobility and 36 for Horatio Alger. Eleven transcripts had "own bootstraps," compared to six, five, and four respectively for social mobility, downward mobility, and economic mobility. One irrelevant hit involving a racehorse named Rags to Riches was discarded.

The transcripts were trimmed to just the story in which the keyword occurred, encompassing everything from anchor toss to any tag elements--including, especially on cable, any discussion segment. The stories were saved as Microsoft Word documents with a separate document for each provider, and all stories having an ending code marker so they could be separated for individual story analysis. The files were entered into some standard programs, WordStat and QDA Miner, for analysis.

Rags-to-riches stories and Horatio Alger tales may be a subset of larger Hero myths or a unique mythology all their own, one heavily intertwined with notions of America and the American Dream. That can be a debate for another day. What strongly emerged, however, was the newscasts presented those mythologies largely in an unchallenged form.

The search terms yielded a total of 187 references in 172 stories. "Rags to riches" was by far the most used of the search terms, appearing 84 times. Most stories merely used the terms in personal narratives about people, often implicitly or explicitly praising both the principle and the people. The fifteen stories with the words downward mobility, social mobility, or economic mobility did, however, take a more serious account of the larger trends.

Those latter fifteen stories did in some way qualify the accepted mythology of upward mobility, if not directly debunk it. Three MSNBC stories presented the harsh recent data on mobility, each time as a challenge to trickle down economics. Fox News casually and incidentally mentioned that neither George W. Bush nor Al Gore were Horatio Alger stories. Otherwise, Fox generally presented the social mobility mythology words unchallenged, especially in telling tales of successful businessmen. Fox and MSNBC both were more likely than the network newscasts to mention rags-to-riches or Horatio Alger in reference to entertainers or political figures. Of particular note was who were presented as a rags-to-riches or Horatio Alger stories.

Rags to Riches, or Horatio Alger References	Networks	Fox	MSNBC
Entertainers	4	8	10
Business persons	10	14	3
Politicians	2	13	15
Other Persons	5	2	5
Non-Persons (ideas, plots, animals, etc.)	12	10	9

"Own bootstraps" was used in a very limited manner. MSNBC and NBC each used a sound bite from then-candidate Barack Obama talking about how Republicans insist on that approach "even if you don't have boots." Fox twice used the same bite. Fox's Neil Cavuto also used "own bootstraps" glowingly in reference to a business owner, as did one NBC report. On MSNBC boxing promoter Don King twice used the phrase in reference to himself. One *Hardball* guest echoed Obama's claim about the phrase, and one critic used it in a disparaging review of the Disney film *American Heart and Soul*. CBS used "own bootstraps" to describe Clarence Thomas' judicial philosophy. ABC and CBS respectively had a painting contractor and a hurricane cleanup volunteer advocating that philosophy and using the phrase.

I also conducted an additional analysis to see what three word phrases also came up in these news stories identified. Some of the most common included: the American people, the American dream, the American public, only in America, millions of dollars, and the middle class. The Republican Party and The Democratic Party also occurred frequently, but only in the MSNBC (13 Democratic, 11 Republican) and Fox transcripts (9 Democratic, 14 Republican) and not at all in those of the network news stories.

These results, combined with those showing a heavy use of rags-to-riches and Horatio Alger references for politicians, document the expected politicization by Fox News and MSNBC. Fox and MSNBC were more likely than the network newscasts to mingle partisan and political themes into social and economic mobility stories. Furthermore, rags-to-riches themes generally were passed along unchallenged, but what little critical debunking occurred happened largely on MSNBC.

One particularly telling moment was on the September

20, 2010, edition of MSNBC's *Hardball.* Host Chris Matthews

seemed stunned about the economic mobility realities being

described by guest Arianna Huffington:

HUFFINGTON: And you know, Chris,
they're not just afraid of the reset. They're living the
reset. A hundred million people in this country are
now living at a standard of living that is not as good
as their parents at the same age. We are number 10 in
upward mobility, you know, behind France and
Germany and (INAUDIBLE) You know, they are
doing...
MATTHEWS: Above France? We're below
France in upward mobility?
HUFFINGTON: We are below France.
Exactly. They're doing the American dream better
than we are. We should...
MATTHEWS: Wait a minute. I thought in
France, you got used to the fact that your father was a
baker, you're a baker. If your grandfather was a
shoemaker, you're a shoemaker. You're telling me
that they're...
HUFFINGTON: Yes.
MATTHEWS: ... they've broken out of that?
HUFFINGTON: I'm telling you these
numbers have changed, and basically now the middle
class life has become a game of chance. If you're
lucky, you'll have a middle class life.

Overall, U. S. television news rather consistently presented a picture of social and economic mobility that repeats and promotes the mythology rather than any questioning of it. The audience largely gets stories praising the life stories of individuals, rather than any mention of the larger trend— namely that such stories are becoming less common and more difficult to achieve, and that the mechanisms for such mobility are under stress.

These findings about television news content complement what others have noted about television entertainment programming. Social class rarely is directly addressed in scripts or storylines, and class representations remain an under-analyzed area. One early tally found that only eleven of the 262 network domestic sitcoms aired between 1946 and 1990 portrayed working-class characters and experiences. Further, between 1955 and 1971 not a single new working-class domestic sitcom appeared on TV. Sitcoms, she noted, tilt toward middle-class and upper-middle-class experiences. Evening dramas often feature the professional class or the hyper-wealthy. The working class now can be found in some daytime talk shows and "reality" programs, but in the latter "exaggerations and rehabilitations of class figure heavily in the premises of these shows."[46]

My tallies found that nationally distributed U. S. television news, network newscasts and cable television reports, generally presented the mythologies of social and economic mobility without complicating the story by mentioning counter-thematic realities. Rags-to-riches, Horatio Alger tales fit the American ethos of who we think we are. Newscasts use that story frame, unmindful or ignoring the substantial evidence it is an unrepresentative and increasingly unlikely tale of who we really are.

My research hardly would have been worth the effort if it merely documented a routine failing in scale, scope, and emphasis of broadcast news coverage of a particular topic. Trade press articles have documented superficial coverage of fleeting spot news events and an array of public policy topics. American notions of rags-to-riches opportunities, however, are key to self-identity, political imperatives, and our understanding

of societal superstructure.

As the Pew Research Center in 2011 pointed out, very

rarely does 90% of the U. S. public line up on any poll question

answer. Yet, 90% of Pew respondents routinely and consistently

agree with the statement "I admire people who get rich by

working hard." Only two other questions consistently received

90% agreement in nearly a quarter-century of Pew political

value surveys. Those two were "I feel it's my duty as a citizen to

always vote" and "It's best for the future of our country to be

active in world affairs."[47]

Significant social, political, and economic questions likely

would emerge if those respondents knew how remote, and

increasingly difficult, the "work hard, get rich" theme really was.

U. S. television news messages have not played a significant role

in that realization; and, in fact, largely perpetuate an increasingly

unlikely mythology.

Chapter 3.   For the Umpteenth Time, Media Aren't Liberal

Over-the-air television dominated the American

entertainment scene in the 1960s and 1970s, and *TV Guide* went

along for the ride. The compact magazine routinely went via

postal delivery or supermarket checkout to the coffee tables of

middle-brow, middle-class, middle America. It was rivaled in

circulation only by the similarly compact *Reader's Digest*, and by

Modern Maturity, then the magazine of the American Association

of Retired People.

In an analog world of three big commercial networks,

cash-fat and happy local affiliates, and fixed-time viewing, *TV*

Guide was a hard-copy planner. The center section was

comprised of hourly program listings, modified by multiple

editions for various TV markets. The slick cover, opening and

closing sections wrapped around those listings, and usually were

light and breezy entertainment fare. Publisher Walter

Annenberg, supporter of conservative Republicans and friend to

Richard Nixon and Ronald Reagan, sometimes let his politics

snarl or growl from the pages—views typically shared by and penned by writer/editor Edith Efron.

Efron's *The News Twisters* is a hodgepodge of coding replete with overlapping categories, categories that omit items, and curious coding choices. The tallying was done by Efron herself, clearly with an eye toward the predetermined conclusion that network TV news in the 1968 presidential campaign tilted toward Humphrey and against Nixon.[48] Four researchers set out to replicate and test her claims, this time using more standard content analysis procedures. They wrote, "There was no evidence of any systematic evaluative bias for or against any of the three candidates [including Wallace]. Coverage of all three candidates was remarkably similar.... Coverage of the three campaigns was also strikingly similar in regard to the issues and campaign activities with which they were identified."[49]

In the spring of 1981 our Syracuse graduate seminar in media issues hosted Reed Irvine, founder of Accuracy in Media (AIM). His prime interest, however, was not accuracy in the usual sense—factual or spelling errors. Instead, he blustered about liberal bias, trying to breathe life into the old Efron canard. His proof was little more than anecdotes; and the class members, even the normally quiet ones, responded with tough questions that Irvine largely deflected into yet more anecdotes and strained assertions. Irvine and AIM, as noted by David Brock in *The Republican Noise Machine*, saw world as just two camps, beneficent capitalism and evil communism. "AIM's original aim was to discredit the media as pro-Communist in the eyes of the public" and also to support Nixon's Vietnam policies, the military coup in Chile, and even charging antiwar protesters with treason, Brock wrote.[50]   I suppose if Irvine stood that far to the right, everything looked left.

Some of use wrote brief response articles, noting the numerous flaws in his arguments, and that a more honest name for his organization would be Conservative Orthodoxy in Media. Our instructor took some exception to me using the word nefarious to describe AIM's activities. I wonder if he'd still object now that corporations are funding even more right-wing groups (or fake think tanks) to flog the liberal media canard, and the claim has become a meme in the right-wing echo chamber.

A few years later one of my former students invited me onto his radio show to challenge Irvine. I was ready and did so. These bogus claims, or more precisely many of these claimants, seem immune to logic, facts, descriptive data, and even well-done studies. One can pile them high and all will be ignored; the same debunked claims will be repeated unchanged to the next audience. The most you will get in reply is yet another anecdote, distraction, or even personal name calling. The so-called liberal media seemed to open many doors for Irvine. By the mid-1980s he had a syndicated column in 100 newspapers and a daily radio commentary on 250 stations.[51]

Irvine sometime in the 1990s was eclipsed in echo chamber parroting by another far-right voice, Brent Bozell. Bozell's Media Research Center started with AIM's mailing list and some of the same wealthy and corporate sponsors. However, where Irvine had rightwing billionaire Richard Mellon Scaife, the Coors Foundation, Mobil Oil and Union Carbide, Bozell found even more such backers and grew to roughly six times the size of AIM. He could put out a daily stream of demands for "balance," a perspective treating all ideas as opinions and demanding numerical parity with no regard for the veracity of the point.[52] Bozell and Brent H. Baker put out a book of collected "research." It was reviewed by longtime *Journalism Quarterly* editor Guido Stempel. The review points out that of the 45 reported studies only a handful give full information on who did the study or how it was done. At least 31 appear to be content analyses, but a key check on the accuracy and validity of that work, coder reliability, never is mentioned.

Stempel also wrote:

> The second reason the book fails is the overall perspective that emerges. While they never say so outright, Bozell and Baker obviously operate from the premise that all statements in the media are opinions. Since there are no facts, expertise is not a matter of concern. What matters is the political leaning of the source, and apparently there are no neutrals. For example, the American Friends Society and the National Audubon Society are liberal.
> What this suggests is that the ideal for a story on the effect of acid rain on birds is to

balance the statement from the Audubon Society person who has a Ph.D. in zoology with one from an American Electric Power office who has an MBA and a C- in high school biology.

Stempel also noted that assertions of bias regarding a topic or news organization often had no coverage comparison groups. He concluded, "What it does not add up to is anything approaching conclusive evidence of liberal bias. However, the book is a serious challenge to those of us who are committed to objective research."[53]

Descriptive data from other sources can provide a clearer picture. *Editor & Publisher* magazine has tracked presidential endorsements since 1940. In only four of those elections (1964, 1992, 2004, and 2008) have a majority of the endorsing daily newspapers opted for the Democratic nominee. For those scoring at home, that's 14 elections where the nation's opinion pages said vote Republican, compared to 4 for Democratic.[54]

Bottom of the ballot endorsements are less often tracked, so from 2002 to 2006 I conducted a massive sampling of them, all endorsements from 20 randomly selected papers in each of

three election years. I found that party breakdown was almost
even, but newspapers favor incumbents more than four to one
over challengers. In congressional endorsements, where I could
use American Conservative Union and Americans for Democratic
Action scoring, endorsed candidates actually were slightly more
conservative than the overall Congress.[55]

Let's remember that freedom of the press belongs to the
man who owns one. It seems unlikely that publishers, barons of
business, would be radical lefties. It's been a while since anyone
tested this point, but the last time a researcher did so 55 percent
of our chain-owned newspaper publishers were Republican, 40
percent were Independents, and only 5 percent as Democratic.[56]

Let's also note that almost every daily newspaper has a
section called Business, but the number of full-time U. S. labor
reporters now can be counted on one hand.[57] What about those
persons whose explicit opinions appear regularly in syndicated
columns? Fairness and Accuracy in Reporting
(www.fair.org/index.php)

has observed that seven of the ten top-circulation syndicated columnists are conservatives. That group also points out that conservatives reign when one looks at the think tanks giving policy opinions in news stories. The top six are either centrist such as Brookings, Rand, or the Council on Foreign Relations or the explicitly conservative Heritage Foundation, American Enterprise Institute, or Center for Strategic and International Studies.

Regarding your radio dial you can check Talkers Magazine's annual list (http://www.talkers.com/heavy-hundred/) to confirm that conservatives outnumber liberals easily four or five to one.

Local television news, something I've been studying since my dissertation, often draws a higher rating in a particular market than its network counterpart half-hour newscast. Further, the dramatic decline in overall network TV audience has been matched by only a small one at the local level.[58] Yet, ownership for a couple decades has pressed local TV newsrooms to do more with less. The result is cheap video (satellite feeds, video news releases, webcams, viewer submissions, internet maps and graphics) and many short stories, a curious mix of crime blotter, disasters and accidents, and "feel good" local charitable events. It also is remarkably apolitical, as documented in tallies started by Rocky Mountain Media Watch and continued by the Lear Center. In the October preceding a November election one is five times more likely to see an ad for a local candidate, than a story involving a local candidate.[59]

Though ownership has concentrated, magazine and book titles have grown substantially and cover the political spectrum; the same could be said of web political offerings. Cable TV has an entire channel, Fox News, devoted 24-hours a day to right-wing views. Business channels such as Fox Business and CNBC can be counted on for corporate reporting that does not challenge overall corporate perspectives. Liberals and progressives can take solace in some programs on MSNBC and Current. That is, if they pay for higher tier cable channels.

The right-wing media complaint largely rests on complaints about individual stories or characterizations of some reporters' personal political preferences—which is a bit like studying auto workers to understand the design of cars, it misses the decision points for broader coverage policies and the establishment of organizational habits and traditions. Former CBS Correspondent Bernard Goldberg has picked up the debunked Efron crusade; he's run with it through a series of books. I had the opportunity to test some of the broader Goldberg claims (network TV homeless coverage by presidential administration, conservative versus liberal source labeling, child care and child well being), and none of them held up to descriptive data scrutiny.[60]

So why is so much effort extended to promote the falsehood that media are liberal? Eric Alterman proffered the reason is "working the refs," the opinion page editors, newscast producers, talk show bookers, etc. The goal would be to extend the right-wing, corporate, and conservative advantage by mainstreaming the false notion of a liberal media.[61]

Alterman likely is correct, but let me suggest several additional reasons. Initially, the liberal media canard provides an easy excuse for right-wing politicians or lawmakers to blame the messenger. The problem isn't that their message is flawed, their votes are contradictory, the motives are suspect, or their policies are failing. Nope. Folks, it's all that damn liberal media.

Secondly, once the liberal media fib becomes a mainstream assumption then competing perspectives are framed outside the acceptable range of debate. Liberals and media professionals alike must go on the defensive (and thus seem like co-conspirators). "No, we're not liberal, or too liberal, or whatever." Edward Herman, Noam Chomsky, and Justin Lewis have pointed out a number of "filters" (ownership, influence of advertising, selective sourcing, and public relations flak) all structurally push established mass media toward conservative and corporate-friendly positions.[62] Yet such observations in our current skewed debate would seem, pun intended, to come out of left field.

A third point is that reducing the debate to a simple left-right scale is simplistic. Not all issues, of course, fit nicely into a liberal versus conservative linear model. Some cross our ideological boundaries; some aren't very political at all. Furthermore, the implicit suggestion is that the biggest problem with journalism is political bias. One could make a stronger case for: superficiality, sensationalism, insufficient original reporting, and blind spots for certain groups, areas, and topics.

Finally, one could look at the prevarication of shouting "liberal media" as part of a larger strategy to discredit in advance the few remaining outlets for non-corporate, anti-plutocratic information. Irvine, in fact, moved onto campus (so to speak) in 1985, creating Accuracy in Academia to harass professors.[63]

Such a news model, ironically touted under the banner fair and balanced, lessens democratic self-governance via honest discussion and deliberation. Instead, we get cheerleading for sides, each hurling at each other unchecked anecdotes and unrestrained personal attacks. Further, such an approach to news diminishes the definition of news for the next generation of reporters, not to mention current and future news audiences. Already I see a disturbing tendency in young people to see news in general and public affairs in particular as difficult, nasty, entirely relative in outlook, and generally unimportant in the lives and unworthy of their time.

A different "Fox News Effect" is taking shape among its frequent viewers. Public opinion polls are beginning to show Fox devotees are quite confident in their answers to news questions, even when those answers are incorrect. Two recent New Jersey polls even discovered that Fox News viewers performed worse than those who fail to follow the news in knowledge of Middle East and North African uprisings or the European debt crisis.[64]

An earlier poll had distressingly similar findings. Program on International Policy Attitudes conducted the poll in January through September 2003. It found that persons who report relying on Fox News had large misperceptions about the Iraq War. Some 80% of Fox News viewers got one or more of three items wrong. Thirty three percent believed that the U.S. has found weapons of mass destruction. Thirty five percent thought global public opinion supported the war. Two-thirds thought the U.S. has found clear evidence Saddam Hussein was working closely with al-Qaeda. The 45% error rate for Fox News viewers was higher than for error rate for viewers of all other broadcast and cable news outlets as well as those who relied on print media.[65]

Let's look specifically at the Fox News slogan Fair and Balanced. Fairness has some merit as a noble goal. It has to be more, however, than a marketing buzz phrase or a twist on the Efron/Irvine/Bozell nonsense, implicitly or explicitly slamming news competitors or appealing to persons who've bought that discredited canard. Fairness implies a broader effort to recognize ones own habits, perspectives, and implicit assumptions and be open to a vast range of alternate sources and topics, yet still applying critical thinking and empirical evaluation to the results. Organizations such as News Hounds and Media Matters routinely report on the failure to achieve this standard in the house of Roger Ailes and Rupert Murdoch, Fox News.

Balance, on the other hand is a false goal, elevated to an unworthy god. Balance would require rough parity of time and respect for a NASA Scientist versus a flat-Earth advocate.

Balance leaves unchallenged the false, calculating, and mean-

spirited claims of death panels in health care laws, or the stale

and disproven challenges to President Obama's birth certificate.

In such a fun-house mirror of a newsroom there are no more

facts, just feelings, perceptions, and opinions on a worn out left-

right scale. Perception becomes certainty. Comedian Steven

Colbert, in his delightful mock character as right-wing host,

dismisses the "brainiacs" and "factinista," and encourages people

to trust their gut, even over observed reality. As he declared in

his fantastic 2006 speech to the White House Correspondents

Dinner, "Realty has a well-known liberal bias."[66]

Stop Corporate Polluters

Wall Street Can't Have My Social Security

Jail Corporate Criminals

Deny Corporate Lies

Corporations Are NOT People

No Corporate Buying of Elections

Fight Corporate Union Busting

Stop Corporate Raids on My Pension

Corporations Aren't Human or Humane

The Corporate Media Blind Spot

Chapter 4. Slurring the Poor and Glorifying the Rich

I grew up in a working-class Pittsburgh neighborhood, old brick homes jammed close to one another and hard against the city line. Our family lived so close to a major thoroughfare that there were parking meters in front of our house. I could walk two blocks to a barbershop, a bowling alley, or either of two bars—all prime hangouts for grumbling old white guys.

You may have encountered the type—dissatisfied with life and feeling shortchanged, blaming not the powerbrokers but the dispossessed. Such grumblers think a huge part of federal spending is welfare and think it is taken from their wallets to give to greedy, cheating, fat, sexually and morally deficient loafers. Racial epithets and stereotypes easily mix into this set of ignorant, inaccurate, and offensive claims, especially if the grumpy speaker feels safe in his company. This grumpy theme has remarkable staying power, seemingly immune to contrary information and even conflicting experience. Instead, it thrives on anecdotes, half-remembered and half-true, as its "proof" of

welfare Cadillacs.[67]

It doesn't help, of course, that some unscrupulous

politicans (often in the pocket or at the behest of great pelf) are

willing to slide into office on a trail of such slime. I write in such

a blunt manner for two reasons. The first is that one can find a

remarkable amount of supporting information for my points.

The second reason is that substantial effort must be exerted to

break this repugnant grumpy-old-conservative-guys meme.

Dozens of surveys have asked respondents why others

are poor. The results are amazingly consistent and statistically

significant across time and culture. I've downloaded many of

those surveys and conducted what researchers call a secondary

analysis. Rather than bore the casual reader with excessive

detail, I've put the results into some convenient, if somewhat

nerdy, tables.[68] The bottom-line conclusions are clear and

compelling. Those who self-identify as conservative or right

wing say others are poor because of personal failings such as

being lazy or drunk. Those who call themselves liberal or left wing say others are poor because of social or economic problems such as low wages and insufficient educational opportunities. A few other factors sometimes (rarely) showed a strong connection to political philosophy, but only religiosity consistently rivaled "why poor/rich" in strength of relationship to left versus right, liberal versus conservative.[69]

Pollsters less frequently ask the inverse question, why are others wealthy? Nevertheless, the same pattern emerges. Conservatives pointed to meritorious personal characteristics such as thrift and hard work. Liberals opt for social and economic explanations such as inheritance and family connections (See Very Nerdy Tables 1-6, if you must).[70]

Of course, people have a compelling need to explain things. These explanations tend to break down into things internal to the self or to an outside force, a phenomenon that academics sometimes call Attribution Theory.[71] This approach fits nicely with George Lakoff's observations that in the U. S. conservatives and Republicans take a "stern father" approach to issues, finding individual fault for almost any problem, while Democrats and liberals look to external forces.[72]

My work on this matter started with dozens of domestic polls and expanded to large international surveys. World Values Survey, for example, asked why people are in need. Those who said those persons are lazy or lack will power averaged 6.07 on the one-to-ten, left-to-right scale, compared to 5.46 for those who blamed an unfair society. The World Values Surveys were a four-wave aggregate, 1982 to 2000, covering more than 250,000 respondents in 80 countries.[73]

Latinobarómetro is an annual public opinion survey, conducted by a non-profit based in Chile. Typically it conducts 19,000 interviews in 18 Latin American countries, representing more than 400 million people. In 2000 asked about the causes of poverty. The 5250 respondents who said poor people do not make much effort scored 5.61 on the same one-to-ten, left-right scale. The 8920 who said poor people exist owing to circumstances averaged 5.15.[74] Both the World Values Survey and Latinobarómetro differences were at a high level of statistical significance.[75]

Other researchers have noticed the same patterns specifically among the British. One researcher studied attitudes toward the poor among respondents in Liverpool and Glasgow, using a Poverty Scale and the Protestant Ethic Scale. He found supporters of the British Conservative Party more likely to blame the poor for their plight. Labour Party supporters were much less likely to do so. Supporters of the Liberal/SDF Alliance fell somewhere in between.[76]

A recent study conducted seven focus groups with 58 members of the English public about wealth taxes. The researcher hoped to counteract the "death taxes" frame on estate taxes with other ways of framing the issue. Participants, however, generally clung to opposition to wealth and inheritance taxes even when presented with substantial contrary information.[77] Similarly a researcher India found those persons with a right-wing orientation exhibit more negative attitudes toward the poor than those with a left-wing orientation.[78]

I also was able to test this pattern using the Polish General Social Survey (Table 6). Recent political crosscurrents in Poland also make the inquiry worth doing. Poland has a unique mythology of wealth that can be found in both its peasant and literary subcultures. Public opinion was fairly negative toward the 1990s burst of wealth accumulation, and attitudes lingered that the Polish business elite used shady practices to obtain and maintain wealth.[79] Poland really has bifurcated into two classes: a small, well-educated urban and upscale group active in civic life; and a poor, rural, dissatisfied class less likely to participate in civic life or to see democracy and universally beneficent.[80]

So it turns out the grumbling old conservative men in Pittsburgh bars, barbershops, and bowling alleys actually represent a broader and culturally universal political pattern. Conservatives blame the poor for their plight; liberals look to social causes. Thus, unified efforts to fight poverty face a huge hurdle. Such an effort came together in President Lyndon Johnson's War on Poverty and Great Society programs. Today's conservatives tend to stereotype those programs as failures. However, a comprehensive review of them, John E. Schwarz's book *America's Hidden Success*, tells a different story. He writes, "The government's programs to attack poverty, though at times seriously flawed, frequently were effective. They reduced

poverty by more than half. They alleviated some of the

grimmest conditions attendant to poverty, and they did so across

the whole range of

human needs....In 1980 one in fifteen Americans faced the

desperation of poverty, compared with one in five Americans

just a generation earlier. This was accomplished, almost

entirely, by the government."[81]

Schwarz properly stresses the government role in

addressing the needs of the poor for education, basic skills, and

job training. He noted that private sector growth only

marginally assists the poor.

Furthermore, work alone is no guarantee against poverty,

as millions

of working poor families today subsisting on the minimum wage

will testify.

In 1981, however, the progress in reducing poverty abruptly

came to an end. The Reagan Administration and its voodoo

economics looked only to private sector solutions--pushing huge tax breaks for the wealthiest and corporations, massive military spending, and severe cutbacks in social programs.

Progressive Democrats were unable to muster two-thirds majorities to overcome actual or threatened presidential vetoes. The executive branch no longer supported the programs it was supposed to administer. The minimum wage was stagnant for years. The gap between the haves and have nots swelled. Instead of outrage, our media lionized Reagan. The Great Prevaricator, of course, left a legacy of scandals including record numbers of members of his administration convicted in court,[82] not to mention a tripling of the national debt.[83]

The grumbling guys in the bars and barbershops take no heed of that history. They continue to argue and to vote against their own interests, good sense, and proven effective programs. They don't seem to notice the strings being pulled to keep their focus on their marginally poorer neighbors; and they never look up to see the locus of the financial abuse.

Chapter 5. Dow Jones v. Tao Jones, Cultivating Consumers not Citizens

I flashback to being twelve years old and trying on pants in the dressing room of Stephen Richard Company, a Pittsburgh retailer. My mother raises her voice from somewhere among the racks of clothing outside. "Is there enough room in the crotch?" she bellows. There is no good response to that question except to add it to family lore about shopping and our youth.

I'd emerge from that dressing room, carefully avoiding the straight pins and shuffling about to find mom; inevitably she'd wandered off to check out some other item. In the late 1970s and 1980s mom even found part-time work in retail, first at Joseph Horne Company and later at Stephen Richard. She even helped me get a stock boy job at the former. During this period the Pittsburgh Steelers rose to Super Bowl success. Even casual fans were wearing t-shirts bearing the names of favorite players like Franco Harris, Lynn Swann, Joe Greene, or Jack Ham. Mom wore one that bore that name of Coach Chuck Noll. At work she put a jacket over most of it. It fell to me to tell her that what was showing to customers was "uck no."

Our family has an elaborate relationship, if somewhat of a split view, on matters of shopping and the retail trade. My sister Pam lives in Central Ohio, but a visit from our cousin Marisa might prompt both gleefully to arrange a pilgrimage to an outlet mall or the closest IKEA—in Cincinnati. Pam speaks longingly of the favorite department store of her youth, Kauffmann's.

My approach to consumer goods is governed by necessity, function, and comfort. I engage in "point-to-point shopping." Go to the store; buy the desired item; leave. I do not browse for the sake of browsing, except online and regarding ideas. My wife shares more of the sentiments of my mother and sister, and keeps me from being too egregiously unfashionable. There certainly may be a gender component to this, and the growing number of "husband benches" in malls and shopping districts seem to support that observation.

Yet, beyond the personal, there are broader and bigger questions at play. Have our developed economies grown too dependent on consumerism? Have our values become too fond

of it? Have our commercial mass media played a slow but steady

role of inculcating those values. A recently invented term,

"affluenza," presents excess craving for material possessions as a

disease or disorder. One book described it as a rapidly

expanding disease of the mind, a "painful, contagious socially-

transmitted condition of overload, debt, anxiety, and waste

resulting from the dogged pursuit of more."[84]

Of course, all media have potential message effects. On

the pages of fashion magazines anorectic cranes stare out

blankly toward increasingly corpulent readers. Newspapers,

before their recent descent, were chock full of advertising

sections. Commercial radio has fallen into a miasma of right-

wing blather, infomercials, play list music, and frequent

commercial breaks. Advertisers constantly seek new ways to

intrude on internet users and to "monetize" content. Yet

television still deserves special attention for its ubiquity in our

recent past and our current lives.

Reporters when doing a story on television's effects loved to talk to George Gerbner. From 1964 to 1989 he pushed the University of Pennsylvania's Annenberg School toward prominence in Communication Theory. He continued to teach and to advocate his ideas about television until his death in 2005. Gerbner's Hungarian accent gave a Dr. Strangelove quality to his bold pronouncements about television violence.

Gerbner's most famous claim was Cultivation Theory, the idea that television was the central cultural arm of our society and thus has a uniquely influential cumulative effect for its main message—which he claimed was violence, often glorified and justified but rarely shown in terms of its devastating aftermath.[85] Gerbner gathered around him several young scholars, but also drew some criticism. He had a spirited debated with Paul Hirsch over the actual meaning of research supposedly supporting Gerbner's claims, especially claims about fearfulness and social alienation.[86]

Recently I began wondering whether Gerbner's biggest error might be in claiming violence as the central message.

Violence is a convenient and non-lingual plot device. A punch in the face is universal, and is understood from Monterrey to Macao, making film and TV distribution convenient. However, even many non-capitalist broadcast operations (state-owned or social democracy models) have commercial content. The great messages of commercial television, whether in the direct advertisements or in the lives of frequently opulent characters, are "buy stuff" and "material goods make you happy."

At the close of the last century and the beginning of this one I was one of a number of researchers plumbing questions along these lines. Juliet Schor discovered that heavy TV viewers tend to overestimate the standards of living enjoyed by others, and report being heavily in debt. She suggested that TV ads leave a lingering and inflated impression of what's normal; the more a person watches TV, the more he or she spends.[87]

Jeffrey Kottler wrote that mass media "help create shared perceptions about what is considered desirable to possess, whether that is a particular article of clothing or even a scent." In fact, Kottler even suggested materialism questions be added to the standard intake questions of therapists.[88] Popular press articles,[89] several books,[90] and even two documentaries[91] assert materialist/consumer values and behaviors overall are negative and are spread by mass media, especially television.

One cross-national study of 1,226 respondents found a two-step link from television viewing to materialism to life dissatisfaction. The link was present clearly in the Chinese, Australian, and U.S. general population samples, but curiously not so in the Canadian, Turkish, and a U.S. student sample.[92] Two researchers studied 250 Dutch children, documenting a link between their Christmas wish lists and heavily advertised products.[93] In later research they claimed that among children life dissatisfaction comes at the end of chain that starts with exposure to ads, this leads to increased purchased requests, and then leads to disappointment when some advertising-induced purchase requests are not granted. They also found that parent-child communication lessened the effects of both child materialism and purchase requests. Nevertheless, it was the relatively high level of TV exposure, and not consumer communication, that made children in low-income families more susceptible to TV ad effects.[94]

The development of materialist personalities should be cause for some concern. One summary of several past surveys declared that materialists tend to be possessive, preferring to own and keep things rather than rent, borrow, or discard. They also envy the possessions of others, and are non-generous in that they do not share with others. Materialists crave social recognition, and link image and popularity to possessions. They also report being less happy overall and less satisfied with their finances.[95]

Indeed, as I ventured into these choppy waters, it increasingly became clear that the strongest correlations for individual viewers were between increasing hours of television viewing and increased life/financial dissatisfaction. I re-analyzed two large databases and sometimes found an association of heavy TV viewing with self-reported materialistic attitudes. The strongest associations were for the importance of having nice things, the importance of having a high income, and in taking care of yourself before others.[96] Later I re-analyzed European and World Values surveys, face-to-face interviews in 69 societies in 50 countries for a total of more than 60,000 respondents. Asking about materialistic or consumerist values yielded inconsistent results, often yielding no association if asked in agree/disagree form, but showing some connection to viewing when one is forced to rank values from a list. It may well be an artifact of socially acceptable answering. Respondents may not be willing to express shallow materialist attitudes to interviewers, but may be more forthcoming with reporting affluenza symptoms such as unhappiness, financial dissatisfaction, and a general sense of life dissatisfaction. Heavy TV viewers, more than two hours daily, were less likely to report being happy, more likely to say they are financially dissatisfied and dissatisfied with life overall. They also were more likely to say that it was important to teach children about thrift, money, savings, and things. As average viewing minutes increased in 46 nations, unhappiness increased, financial satisfaction and life satisfaction decreased.[97]

In fact, what I had discovered updated and fit nicely with a 1993 combination of seven studies testing a total of 39 hypotheses. Those researchers found that consistently across all studies greater materialism was associated with decreased life satisfaction.[98] So I decided next to graph these relationships using the U. S. General Social Survey (see Tables 7 to 10; they are really not that scary).[99] With the sole exception of satisfaction with family life one sees a clear and significant pattern. As TV viewing increased, so did dissatisfaction with numerous aspects of one's life and finances.

Of course, correlation is not causation; it is possible some missing third variable leads to both heavy TV viewing and affluenza symptoms. (For the statistically sophisticated, I put the data through the rigor of a multiple regression, and the relationship survived, but lost some explanatory power to other contenders regarding the connection). So how should one interpret the low-level but rather persistent and consistent connection between amount of TV viewing and affluenza symptoms?

One could argue for an effects model, namely that heavy TV viewing inculcates materialist values and thus leads to related symptoms. However, one also could look at these findings through the prism of audience uses and gratifications. Those persons already bored, unhappy and financially distressed simply drift toward TV as a cheap and easy form of diversion, companionship, or killing time. This linking of affluenza symptoms to audience needs and habits best fits both the results of this study and the bulk of past work.

Then again, a nuanced and promising approach is to look at these results as documenting one stage in a reinforcing cycle or spiral. Television often presents us with a shiny, fast-paced narrative in which the central figures often are wealthier and thinner than those attracted to the programming. The programs are interrupted with more direct commercials, often stating that the solution to some personal problem is through material goods. When reality fails to live up to this narrative, some viewers get upset not at the message or the medium but at the reality. These viewers thus escape to TV fantasies for yet another cycle of materialism messages.

This point fits well the lament of a quartet of researchers about how the social construction of reality works for many viewers. "The overwhelming conclusion," they wrote, "is that the media generally operate in ways that promote apathy, cynicism, and quiescence rather than active citizenship and participation."[100] Certainly one can find intellectual forerunners to this idea. As early as 1899 Thorstein Veblen coined the expression "conspicuous consumption" to describe how the wealthy use material goods to signal status.[101] The same idea tracks through prominent books like Vance Packard's *The Status Seekers* and John Kenneth Galbraith's *The Affluent Society*.[102] A recent extrapolation went so far as to claim the value of human beings is being reduced to the labels on our shirts; the wishes of ghetto youth for expensive brand-name clothing are a logical result of a dehumanizing materialism.[103]

One model that could inspire healthy debate puts materialistic messages as part of the typical content of established media. Messages more challenging to the status quo are rare, but are more numerous during times of significant social upheaval or in new forms not yet co-opted by political and economic powers.

The typical mediated message thus contains a conflict between the attractive fantasy of the message and the experienced reality of the vast majority of readers, listeners, or viewers. That audience, however, is neither a sponge accepting all messages nor a perpetually alert activist questioning all messages that reach him or her.

A small audience percentage resolves the aforementioned cognitive dissonance actively by being critical of many messages, seeking alternate messages on the fringes of media content, and even creating messages themselves. This sets off a healthy upward cycle of critical thinking, self-empowerment, and organization for change.

A much larger percentage, however, resolves this cognitive dissonance passively by getting upset at the reality. Apathetic and depressed, these viewers default to a use of time that only brings them into contact with more

establishment/materialistic messages. Thus, a negative cycle of

affluenza symptoms becomes self-sustaining.

A Cyclical Model of Media Materialistic Messages

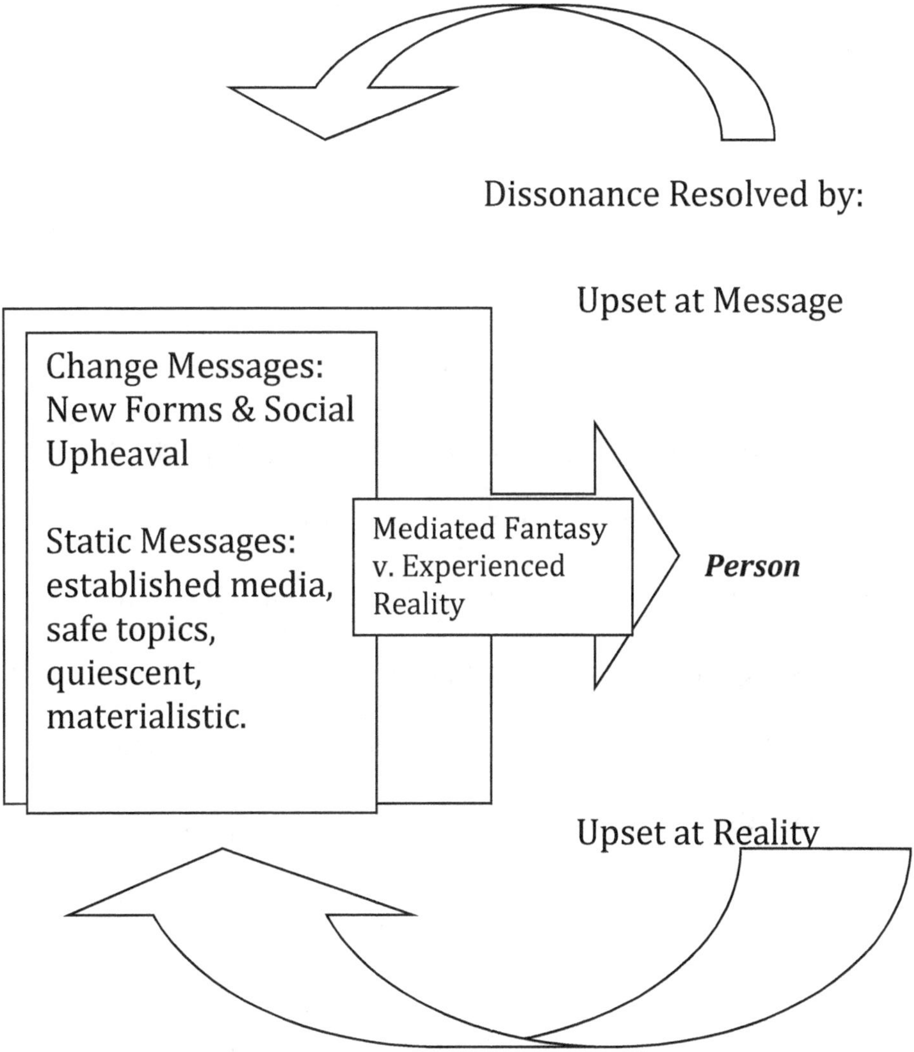

Dissonance Resolved by:

Upset at Message

Change Messages:
New Forms & Social
Upheaval

Static Messages:
established media,
safe topics,
quiescent,
materialistic.

Mediated Fantasy
v. Experienced
Reality

Person

Upset at Reality

Once I put my graduate students to work on a group exercise about developmental communications, the notion that communication resources can be used to spur a country's growth. I gave one group Haiti whose problems included disease and poverty. I gave another Indonesia; it's far-flung geography and multiple languages presented obstacles.

One group had Bhutan, a tny mountain country in the Himalayas, a place uniquely committed to a national goal of Gross National Happiness instead of Gross National Product.[104] The students seemed perplexed about that one, derisively dismissing it as "whatever that means."

"Whatever that means?!" exploded my inner monologue. It means there's so much more to life than money. It means growth is no panacea—and can be devastating if done badly on a planet of seven billion people. I held back, saying something like "I wouldn't dismiss it. That's their goal and part of their Buddhist tradition." Clearly my students had spent more time in the mall than in meditation. Every day the news tells them about Dow Jones, does it ever give them a Tao Jones report?

Chapter 6. Election 2012: No Time for Reversible Mittens

The Stephanie Miller Show is a welcome respite on the radio

dial, a place that not only disputes the usual right-wing blather but

also makes fun of it. In my community and many others her

program must be found online or on Current TV. She, her regulars,

and her callers often refer to the 2012 Republican Party presidential

nominee as Mittens, or Reversible Mittens—a reminder of his

numerous flip-flops on issues. Mitt Romney seems to be running a

campaign devoid of specifics, long on generalities, and backed by a

treasure chest larger than that of the incumbent (a first).

As this campaign kicks into high gear money is at the heart

of all. Romney's campaign is based almost entirely on public

dissatisfaction with the slow pace of economic recovery under

President Obama. The president's campaign fires back that his

opponent proposes nothing but a return to failed policies. Romney

has a net worth estimated at $230 million, double that of the last

eight presidents combined. He is proposing little more than the same

trickle-down policies that benefit him and the extremely wealthy—

and have failed twice already, under Reagan & Bush the Elder and once again under Bush the Lesser.

Romney's reply often is replete with misquotes and factual errors, but largely boils down to a media advertising blitz relying on the buzz words associating wealth with success and shouting "class warfare." Funny how that term is applied only when someone is pointing out that the wealthy are stacking the economic deck. The entire campaign is a virtue case study in the media money myths at the heart of this book. Clearly the occasion merits a discussion about rich people and whether we can sustain the political, social, and economic costs of coddling a small number of people, like Romney, in great and growing wealth.

One hates to stereotype, but rich people have demonstrated a growing sense of entitlement. As noted earlier, I'm not citing that term in its current misuse, as a vague collective for Medicare, Social Security, or unemployment payments. Such programs one pays into, so one is indeed entitled to those benefits.

Instead, our wealthy continue to insist on a system of special privileges: legacy admissions to elite colleges, the passing of massive fortunes undiluted by estate tax from generation to generation, overseas tax shelters like Romney's, and special lower tax rates for their major source of income (capital gains) as compared to the rates applied to wealth the rest of us generate by working hard and smart for wages and salaries.

Rich people also are responsible for a disproportionate share of crime in the suites. We're less than four years removed from a financial meltdown precipitated by wealthy investment firms treating our mortgages as casino chips. Those self-paid millionaires and billionaires made big and dumb bets, secure in the rules they'd rigged so profits were maximized and losses socialized.

U. S. social and economic mobility now has slipped behind all, or nearly all, developed nations. One must feel sorry for the children raised in such a society, including wealthy children like young Willard Mitt Romney trapped in a generation-to-generation cycle of grinding pelf, and its values-challenged environment.

Our wealthiest tend to self-isolate in gated ghettos, exclusive schools, and restricted clubs. There they have little interaction with the vast majority of their fellow citizens. One supposes this makes it easier to depress their wages, denigrate their work effort, and export their jobs a la Bain Capital. It also can lead to an inflated sense of self curiously paired with generational decline.

One cannot know for certain how many trust fund babies genuinely see themselves as "job creators" and how many recognize that as a Frank Luntz buzz phrase designed for politicians being rented by the rich, the sycophants on the editorial pages of the *Wall Street Journal*, and the rubes being bamboozled by Fox News. It is scary to think that some uber-wealthy actually have been drinking the Kool Aid, and think that jobs pour forth like sunshine from every orifice of their body. Of course, our national and community resources and laws make possible the acquisition of wealth, not to mention the crucial roles played by small businesses and the vast majority of us who earn a living by working for someone else.

Generational decline is perhaps best illustrated by one prominent family. Prescott Bush, a son of wealth and privilege, became a banker and later a U. S. Senator. His life and career had positives and negatives, but included admirable moments including service in World War I, work as national campaign treasurer for Planned Parenthood, and the censure of Senator Joseph McCarthy for McCarthy's divisive and abusive practices. Prescott's son,

George Herbert Walker Bush, started promisingly as a courageous World War II pilot, but later in life jettisoned his principles for political gain. He finished his career as the president who pardoned the men capable of implicating him in the Iran-Contra crimes.

By the time one reaches the third generation, George Walker Bush, one finds a man "doomed to succeed," consistently rescued by family friends from lackluster school performance, Vietnam draft status, failed businesses, and a shaky claim to presidential election. Thus, it was not surprising he left the office with a record for vacation days, took the nation from budget surplus to record deficits, put two wars on our national credit card, and left the economy dangling off a cliff.

Yet for all these horrific examples I remain confident in our ability to reintegrate the malefactors of great wealth back into a civil society. We have positive role models in Franklin D. Roosevelt, John F. Kennedy, and Warren Buffett. Each came from or acquired great wealth, and each has demonstrated concern for equitable public policy, opportunity for all in the next generation, and compassion for the impoverished.

The societal re-integration of the super-rich must start with taxes. This year the Social Security cap out is $110,100. After that in yearly income, no more Social Security tax. Most of us never reach that total in a typical year, but that figure is less than the yearly bonus, let alone the generous salary, of an executive at Chase or Goldman and several other Wall Street firms or prominent transnational corporations. That cap should be eliminated so the rich help secure the future of Social Security, instead of advancing ideas that change it into a steadily-devalued coupon given to grandma to seek the tender mercies of the insurance industry. Inheritance taxes should be maintained. Capital gains and earned income should be treated the same for tax purposes.

At this writing Mitt Romney is dismissing the growing calls to release a significant amount his income tax forms. He refuses to match the disclosure pattern of his father George Romney. The elder Romney released twelve years of tax records during his 1968 run for the presidency. Reversible Mittens will not release the tax records he made available to Senator John McCain when the latter four years ago was screening potential running mates.

A national return to progressive taxes, ones that rise with ability to pay, not only will help with needed infrastructure/job programs but also will reduce deficits. Further, such a change would put us back in the same society, recognizing we are all in this together. President Obama has sought, against virulent congressional opposition, some policies that modestly nudge us in that direction. Or course, this process must begin at the polls— namely by electing candidates who recognize this necessity. Any one who dismisses such needed changes as "class warfare" or advocates a return to "wealthy coddling trickle down," should be regarded as a non-serious and decidedly dangerous candidate.

The stakes couldn't be much higher, as Daron Acemoglu and James A. Robinson chronicled in a sprawling historical review. They document that a stagnant class structure works hand-in-glove with corrupt political cultures and extractive economies in which the work of many is exploited by a privileged elite. Innovation declines and political repression increases. Another long-term consequence is reflected in the book's title, *Why Nations Fail*.[105]

Chapter 7. People Take the Steering Wheel

Hard copy editions of books are static, so the specific numbers in this one eventually may need updating. The larger points, however, should have some staying power. Media technologies change. Consumer habits change. Human nature changes very slowly, as does human behavior within our institutions.

The nerdy academic term for it is Political Economy of Communication. The idea has a lot of explanatory power or the developments reviewed in this book. Every society has three defining characteristics—polity, who can do what to whom and get away with it; economy, who does what and who gets what; and communication, an exchange of messages to keep the other two functioning.

Power thus is fungible; it can move from one to another. The politically well connected can use those connections to acquire wealth and to influence widely communicated messages. The wealthy can influence politicians and policy as well as generate widely distributed messages. Those who own and control communication resources gain wealth and political power.

Then by definition mass and established media drift toward the conservative, the corporate, and the safe. Challenging, liberal, anti-corporate, and anti-plutocratic messages find homes in new media and in distant corners of established media.

Established corporate power finds it advantageous that great numbers of people misunderstand the actual political direction of messages. That some power structure benefits when Horatio Alger rags-to-riches mythologies are trumpeted even as actual economic mobility decreases, and avenues for it wither away.

Mediated messages also can exacerbate the conservative misdirection of associating wealth with noble values and poverty with persona failings. Too often we are exhorted to sneer at our neighbors or at those just slightly worse off than we are. Rarely are we directed to look up and see greed, white collar crime, and ne'er do well trust fund babies.

Finally, power players also benefit when central media messages are "buy stuff," and we see ourselves more as consumers than as citizens.

Pointing out these phenomena can yield interesting reactions—and I've experienced a lot of those reactions in my roles as professor, columnist, and county commissioner. Once I had a Media & Society class read an old *Nation* article that envisioned, generally favorably, the first day in America following a ban on commercial advertising.[106]

Student reaction generally was thoughtful and reflective, but one advertising major was near apoplectic with rage—red faced and calling the article's author a communist.

Sometimes I could prompt perplexed looks by mentioning that we have commercial television and non-commercial television, but where is the anti-commercial television? I'd show various anti-commercial mock ads from Ad Busters, then go to the website for National Buy Nothing Day. The latter occurs on the Friday after Thanksgiving—rarely getting even a TV news ripple in the tidal wave of "blockbuster shopping day" stories.

Public relations students, and some faculty, also may roll their eyes when I get into the darker side of PR. It's not all or even mostly balloon launches for worthy charities. *Toxic Sludge is Good for You*, a notable book and video, gets into opinion-for-hire think tanks, push polls, stacked deck congressional hearings, Astroturf lobbying (aka fake grass roots), and video news releases creeping into newscasts, satellite feeds, and websites.[107]

Recent e-mails to me about my columns on local politics have presented similar name calling, one even invoked the long-discredited Efron and Goldberg assertions. Such are the hisses and groans when a fatuous bubble starts losing air. Friends, it is okay to challenge false memes. Messages promoting the powerful are not the same as powerful messages.

It is perfectly acceptable, and quite good, to notice that the biggest problem with any free market argument is the assumption there is a free market. Further, we do our society and our country a favor when we notice that, despite mediated distractions, we are moving away from our noblest principles (opportunity, respect, peace, justice, fair systems) instead of toward them.

A 1964 Hertz rental car commercial featured the visual effect of a seated man and woman floating on air, drifting into the front seat of a jazzy convertible.[108] The announcer declared, "Let Hertz put you in the driver's seat." Let's work again toward that restrained, moderate, and reasonable day when corporations put us in the driver's seat and don't try to grab the steering wheel.

Table 1. Eurobarometer 67.1, 2007. Multiple Regression.
Political Views v. "Why Poor/Rich" and Other Independent
Variables.

Variable	B	Std. Error	Beta	t	P
YPSVP	.144	.016	.076	8.792	.000
Attachment to Country	-.272	.034	-.082	-7.882	.000
Attachment to World	.134	.026	.055	5.206	.000
Attachment to Europe	-.146	.030	-.054	-4.903	.000
Feeling Fulfilled in Professional Life	-.090	.026	-.035	-3.449	.001
Type of Community	-.059	.024	-.021	-2.479	.013
Age	-.002	.001	-.015	-1.753	.080
Personal Import-ance of Culture	.040	.024	.015	1.653	.098
Level of Education	-.003	.004	-.007	-.820	.412
Attachment to Town/Village	.015	.034	.005	.439	.661
Attachment to Region	.010	.036	.003	.275	.783
Feeling of Fulfilled Private Life	-.004	.030	-.001	-.146	.884

Valid N = 13,617; Adjusted R squared .018. In all tables
YPSVP is shorthand for Why Poor Social versus Personal

Table 2. International Social Justice Project, 1996 and 2000.
Political Views v. "Why Poor/Rich" and Other Independent
Variables.

Variable	B	Std. Error	Beta	t	P
Govt. Does Right Thing	.293	.053	.140	5.531	.000
YPSVP	.072	.014	.132	5.266	.000
Politicians Do Not Care	.131	.041	.081	3.197	.001
Age	.006	.003	.058	2.069	.039
Education, Years of Schooling	-.049	.027	-.051	-1.84	.068
Freq. Attend Religious Services	-.049	.036	-.034	-1.340	.181
Reads Newspaper	.049	.050	.025	.978	.328
Household Income	-7.936	.000	-.022	-.869	.385
Size of Community	-.005	.021	-.006	-.225	.822

Valid N = 1547; Adjusted R squared .042

Table 3. International Social Justice Project, 1991.
Political Views v. "Why Poor/Rich" and Other Independent
Variables.

Variable	B	Std. Error	Beta	t	P
YPSVP	.055	.008	.141	7.215	.000
Freq. of Attending Religious Services	-.143	.024	-.111	-6.012	.000
Government Does the Right Thing	-.237	.053	-.114	-4.516	.000
Age	.009	.003	.055	2.948	.003
Same Chance of a Fair Trial	-.050	.026	-.039	-1.933	.053
Satisfaction with Living Standard	-.058	.031	-.050	-1.858	.063
Class	.071	.049	.029	1.468	.142
Satisfaction with Political System	.024	.025	.022	.979	.328
Government for the Benefit of All	-.048	.051	-.024	-.944	.345
Politicians Do Not Care	-.023	.031	-.015	-.754	.451
Voters Have a Real Choice	.014	.029	.010	.480	.631
Satisfaction with Income	-.008	.026	-.007	-.294	.769
Household Income	3.180	.000	.005	.273	.785
Overall Satisfaction	.003	.032	.002	.091	.927
Job Satisfaction	.001	.024	.001	.035	.972

Valid N = 2802; Adjusted R squared .065.

Table 4. International Social Survey Program (ISSP) on Social Inequality, 1992. Political Views v. "Why Poor/Rich" and Other Independent Variables.

Variable	B	Std. Error	Beta	t	P
Freq. of Attending Religious Services	-.097	.022	-.157	-4.500	.000
YPSVP	-.037	.011	-.112	-3.285	.001
Age	.010	.003	.102	2.859	.004
Size of Community	.064	.022	.101	2.895	.004
Family Income	5.052	.000	.166	2.791	.005
Number Hours Worked in Week	.003	.003	.046	1.235	.217
Respondent Earnings	-1.754	.000	-.045	-.723	.470
Education	-.007	.013	-.021	-.545	.586

Valid N = 772; Adjusted R squared .109

Table 5. Polish General Social Survey, 1997, 1999, 2002.
Multiple Regression.
Political Views v. "Why Poor/Rich" and Other Independent
Variables.

Variable	B	Std. Error	Beta	t	P
Feelings About Communism	-.492	.097	-.196	-5.097	.000
Frequency of Religious Attendance	.161	.040	.165	4.071	.000
YPSVP	.059	.017	.130	3.441	.001
Strength Relig. Affiliation	-.702	.213	-.129	-3.287	.001
Total Family Income	.000	.000	-.134	-2.593	.010
Father's Highest Degree	.094	.055	.096	1.724	.085
Satisfaction with Financial Sit.	-.119	.132	-.038	-.900	.368
Age	-.007	.008	-.036	-.885	.377
Respondent Income	9.390	.000	.040	.753	.452
Job Status Higher than Father	-.056	.081	-.030	-.693	.489
Subjective Class Identification	.065	.115	.024	.568	.570
No. Hours Worked in Average Week	.003	.006	.022	.566	.572
Interest in Politics	-.046	.093	-.019	-.490	.625
Mother's Highest Degree	-.003	.058	-.003	-.058	.953

Valid N = 649; Adjusted R squared .136.

Table 6. U. S. General Social Survey, 1990. Multiple Regression Political Views v. "Why Poor/Rich" and Other Independent Variables,

Variable	B	Std. Error	Beta	t	P
Views regarding Homosexual Sex	-.293	.048	-.230	-6.114	.000
YPSVP	.163	.033	.184	4.879	.000
Frequency of Religious Attendance	.070	.018	.134	3.831	.000
Age	.004	.003	.044	1.236	.220
Satisfaction with Financial Situation	.060	.068	.032	.890	.376
Income	-.016	.021	-.027	-.738	.463
Happiness	-.028	.085	-.012	-.331	.742
Size of Community	.000	.000	-.028	-.281	.779
Education	-.005	.020	-.011	-.252	.802

Valid N= 746; Adjusted R squared .140.

Table 7. Happiness by Daily TV Hours Viewed

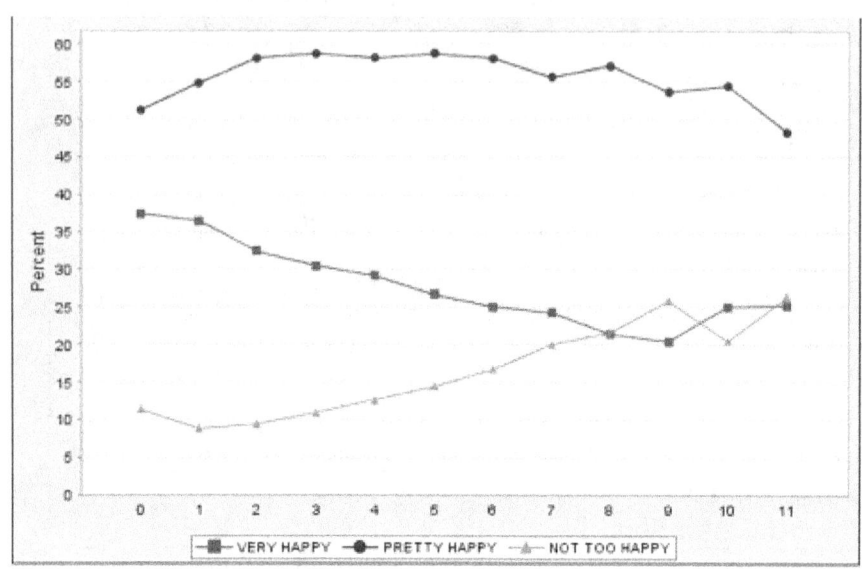

Table 8. Change in Financial Situation by Daily TV Hours Viewed

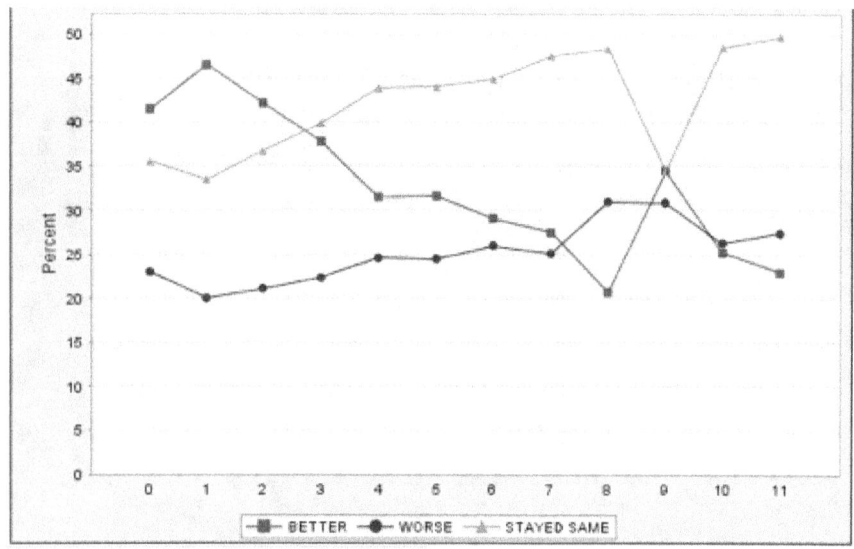

Table 9. Financial Satisfaction by Daily TV Hours Viewed

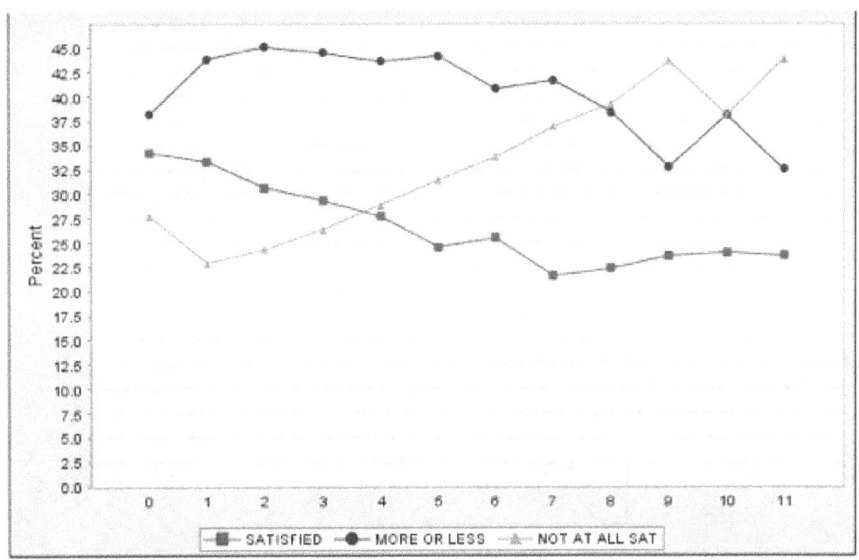

Note: All figures were calculated on the full 0-to24-hours scale for TV viewing. For clarity and ease of reading, this chart collapses the small set of upper-end responses into an eleven-plus hours category.

Table 10. Daily TV Hours by Five Measures of Satisfaction in

One's Life

	Very Great (All) Sample Size	Great Deal	Quite a Bit	Fair Amt.	Some	Little	None
Hobbies	2.74 (2.98) 14,083	2.79	2.95	3.23	3.30	3.65	4.15
Friendships	2.81 (2.98) 14,137	2.92	2.99	3.33	3.36	3.83	4.21
Health	2.77 (2.98) 14,121	2.83	2.89	3.25	3.39	3.75	4.31
City/Place	2.98 (2.98) 14,131	2.83	2.84	3.13	3.11	3.36	3.46
Family Life	2.93 (2.98) 14,089	3.01	2.99	3.05	2.99	3.22	3.17

End Notes

---

[1] Morton Mintz and Jerry S. Cohen. *America, Inc.: who owns and operates the United States.* New York: Dial Press, 1971.

[2] Edward Jay Epstein. *News from Nowhere: television and the news.* New York: Random House, 1973; Morton Mintz and Jerry S. Cohen, *Power, Inc.: public and private rulers and how to make them accountable.* New York: Viking Press, 1976; Ben H. Bagdikian. *The Media Monopoly.* Boston, MA: Beacon Press, 1983; Howard Zinn. *A People's History of the United States.* New York: Harper & Row, 1980; Glasgow University Media Group. *Bad News.* London, UK: Routledge and Kegan Paul, 1976.

[3] Mark D. Harmon. *Crashing the Commission: Confessions of a University Twit.* Oak Ridge, TN: Tellico Books, 2011.

[4] Pat Garofalo, "Walmart Heirs Have As Much Wealth As Bottom 40 Percent Of Americans Combined," *Think Progress*, July 17, 2012, using Federal Reserve Data, http://thinkprogress.org/economy/2012/07/17/534591/walmart-heirs-wealth-combined/. See also Pat Garofalo, "The Walmart Heirs Have The Same New Worth As The Bottom 30 Percent Of Americans," *Think Progress*, December 9, 2011, using Survey of Consumer Finances, Forbes, and Congressional Budget Office. http://thinkprogress.org/economy/2011/12/09/385941/walmart-heirs-worth-30-percent-bottom/ Dan Froomkin, "Half Of American Households Hold 1 Percent Of Wealth," *Huffington Post*, posted and viewed July 19, 2012, http://www.huffingtonpost.com/2012/07/19/households-wealth-american-1-percent_n_1687015.html

[5] Joseph E. Stiglitz. *The Price of Inequality: How Today's Divided Society Endangers Our Future.* New York: W. W. Norton & Company, 2012, as previewed in http://truth-out.org/news/item/9891-joseph-e-stiglitz-the-price-of-

inequality
Project Syndicate, News Analysis. Posted June 20, 2012. Viewed July 22, 2012.

[6] OECD, "A Family Affair: Intergenerational Social Mobility across OECD Countries," Chapter 5 in *Economic Policy Reforms 2010: Going for*
Growth, OECD Publishing, 2010, doi: 10.1787/growth-2010-en, 181.

[7] Tom Hertz. Understanding Mobility in America. Washington, DC: Center for American Progress, April 26, 2006, pp. 1-44.; Ron Haskins, "Education and Economic Mobility," Chapter 8 in *Economic Mobility Project*, an Initiative of The Pew Charitable Trusts, downloaded pdf file, 2008. Viewed March 17, 2011. http://www.economicmobility.org/reports_and_research/other?id=00 03.

[8] Joydeep Roy, "Low Income hinders college attendance for even the highest achieving students," Economic Policy Institute, 1-2. http:www.epi.org/economic_snapshots/entry/webfeatures_snapshots 20051012/, October 12, 2005, viewed January 30, 2011.

[9] Nathan D. Martin and Kenneth I. Spenner, "Captial Conversion and Accumulation: A Social Portrait of Legacies at an Elite University," *Research in Higher Education, 50* (7), pp. 623-648.

[10] Rachel Maddow. *Drift.* New York: Crown Publishers, 2012.

[11] AFL-CIO Executive Paywatch, using Securities and Exchange Commission filings, http://www.aflcio.org/Corporate-Watch/CEO-Pay-and-the-99. Viewed July 18, 2012.

[12] Veronique de Rugy, "World's Top Military Spenders: U. S. Spends More than Next Top 14 Countries Combined," Mercatus Center, George Mason University, Dec. 9, 2011. Viewed July 21,

2012. http://mercatus.org/publication/worlds-top-military-spenders-us-spends-more-next-top-14-countries-combined
Also see
http://www.politifact.com/ohio/statements/2011/dec/05/alan-simpson/alan-simpson-says-us-military-spending-outpaces-to/

[13] Barbara W. Tuchman. *The Proud Tower*. New York: Ballantine Books, 1962, p. 386.

[14] Malcolm Forbes. *They Went That-a-Way*. New York: Ballantine Books, 1988, pp. 17-18.

[15] Ralph D. Gardner. Introduction to Horatio Alger's *A Fancy of Hers and The Disagreeable Woman: Two lost novels for adults by the man loved for his rags-to-riches tales for juveniles.* New York: Van Nostrand Reinhold, Co., 1981, p. 5; Gary Scharnhorst with Jack Bales. *The Lost Life of Horatio Alger, Jr.* Bloomington, Indiana: Indiana University Press, 1985, p. 156.

[16] Gardner, 1981, p. 6; Edwin P. Hoyt. *Horatio's Boys: The Life and Works of Horatio Alger, Jr.* Radnor, Pennsylvania: Chilton Book Co., 1974, p. 235.

[17] Frank Gruber. *Horatio Alger, Jr., a Biography and Bibliography.* West Los Angeles, California: Grover Jones Press, 1960, p. 10.

[18] Hoyt, pp. 232, 248.

[19] John Tebbel. *From Rags to Riches: Horatio Alger, Jr., and The American Dream.* New York: The Macmillan Co., 1963, p. 223.

[20] Tebbel, p. 210.

[21] "Horatio Alger Is an Unknown to 92% of Boys and Girls in Seven Clubs in City. *New York Times*, Jan. 13, 1947, p. 23.

[22] Ralph D. Gardner. *Horatio Alger, or the American Hero Era.*

New York: Arco Publishing Co., 1978, p. 344.

[23] Carol Nackenoff. *The Fictional Republic: Horatio Alger and American Political Discourse.* New York: Oxford University Press, 1994.

[24] Scharnhorst and Bales, pp. 64-67; Nackenoff, pp. 20-22; Hoyt, pp. 60-63.

[25] Gardner, 1981, pp. 7-12.

[26] Hoyt, pp. 60-63; Nackenoff, pp. 21-22.

[27] Scharnhorst and Bales, pp. 127-130.

[28] Scharnhorst and Bales, p. 127.

[29] Jack Lule. *Daily News, Eternal Stories: The Mythological Role of Journalism.* New York: Guilford Press, 2001.

[30] OECD, 2010. "A Family Affair: Intergenerational Social Mobility across OECD Countries," Chapter 5 in *Economic Policy Reforms 2010: Going for Growth*, OECD Publishing, doi: 10.1787/growth-2010-en, p. 181.

[31] Miles Corak, ed. *Generational Income Mobility in North America and Europe.* Cambridge: Cambridge University Press, 2004; Miles Corak, "Do Poor Children Become Poor Adults? Lessons from a Cross Country Comparison of Generational Earnings Mobility." IZA Discussion Paper No. 1993. Bonn, Germany: Institute for the Study of Labor, 2006; Julia B. Isaacs., Isabel V. Sawhill, and Ron Haskins. *Getting Ahead or Losing Ground: Economic Mobility in America.* Washington, D.C: The Brookings Institution and the Economic Mobility Project, an Initiative of The Pew Charitable Trusts, 2008; Markus Jäntti, Brent Bratsberg, Knut Roed, Oddbjörn Rauum et al. "American Exceptionalism in a New Light: A Comparison of Intergenerational Earnings Mobility in the Nordic

Countries, the United Kingdom and the United States."
IZA Discussion Paper No. 1938. Bonn: Institute for the Study of
Labor, 2006.

[32] Isaacs, Sawhill, and Haskins, p. 19.

[33] Isaacs, Sawhill, and Haskins, p. 32.

[34] Isaacs, Sawhill, and Haskins, pp. 41-42.

[35] Tom Hertz. Understanding Mobility in America. Washington,
DC: Center for American Progress, April 26, 2006, pp. 1-44.

[36] Isaacs, Sahill and Haskins, pp. 9, 68. Also see Isabel Sawhill
and John E. Morton (2008, February). "Economic Mobility: Is the
American Dream Alive and Well?" Economic Mobility Project, an
Initiative of The Pew Charitable Trusts, downloaded pdf file.
http://www.economicmobility.org/reports_and_research/other
?id=0003. Viewed March 17, 2011, p. 5.

[37] Michael Moore. "Inside Story: Face it, you'll never be rich:
Why do Americans still believe in the rags-to-riches fairy tale?"
The Guardian, Oct. 7, 2003, p. 6.

[38] Pew Economic Mobility and the American Dream Survey.
Conducted by Greenberg Quinlan Rosner Research & Public
Opinion Strategies, January 27 - February 8, 2009 and based on
2,119 telephone interviews. Sample: national adult with
oversamples of blacks, Hispanics and youth under age 40.
Results were weighted to be representative of a national adult
population. [USGREEN.09ECONM. R18]
http://www.ropercenter.uconn.edu/data_access/ipoll/ipoll.htm
l. Retrieved January 2, 2011, from the iPOLL Databank, The
Roper Center for Public Opinion Research, University of
Connecticut.

[39] CBS News/New York Times Poll (1981). Conducted by CBS

News, April 22 - 26, 1981, and based on 1,439 telephone interviews. Sample: national adult. [USCBSNYT.050281.R36]; CBS News/New York Times Poll (1983). Conducted by CBS News, January 16-19, 1983, and based on 1,597 telephone interviews. Sample: national adult. [USCBSNYT.020183.R17; CBS News/New York Times Poll (1988). Conducted by CBS News, July 31 – August 3, 1988 and based on 1,353 telephone interviews. Sample: national adult. [USCBSNYT.080688.R42]; CBS News/New York Times Poll (1996). Conducted by CBS News, February 22 - 24, 1996, and based on 1,223 telephone interviews. Sample: national adult. [USCBSNYT.96002A.Q34]; CBS News/New York Times Poll (1996). Conducted by CBS News, March 20 -21, 1996, and based on 1,001 telephone interviews. Sample: national adult. [USCBS.96003B.Q01]; New York Times Poll (1998). Conducted by New York Times, April 15-20, 1998, and based on 1,395 telephone interviews. Sample: national adult with an oversample of Jews; CBS News/New York Times Poll (2000). Conducted by CBS News, February 6 - 10, 2000 and based on 1,499 telephone interviews. Sample: national adult. [USCBS.200002A.Q07]; CBS News/New York Times Poll (2003). Conducted by CBS News/New York Times, July 13 - 27, 2003 and based on 3,092 telephone interviews. Sample: national adult with an oversample of Hispanics (see note). The sample included 2008 non-Hispanics and 1074 Hispanics. Results are weighted to reflect the actual ethnic distribution of the US population. [USCBSNYT.080503.R14]; CBS News/New York Times Poll (2007). Conducted by CBS News, June 26 - 28, 2007 and based on 836 telephone interviews. Sample: national adult. [USCBS.070107.R72]; CBS News/New York Times Poll (2009). Conducted by CBS News/New York Times, April 1 - 5, 2009 and based on 998 telephone interviews. Sample: national adult. The interviews were conducted by land-line and cell phones. [USCBSNYT.040609.R16]. All Retrieved in 2011 (Jan. 2, 24, March 17 and 21), from the iPOLL Databank, The Roper Center for Public Opinion Research, University of Connecticut. http://www.ropercenter.uconn.edu/data_access/ipoll/ipoll.html.

[40] Stephen J. McNamee and Robert K. Miller, Jr. (2004). The Meritocracy Myth. Lanham, Maryland: Rowman and Littlefield Publishers, Inc., 2004, p. 45.

[41] Allan Ornstein. *Class Counts: Education, Inequality, and the Shrinking Middle Class.* Lanham, Maryland: Rowman and Littlefield Publishers, Inc., 2007, p. 100.

[42] Don Heider and Koji Fuse, "Class and Local TV News," Chapter 5 in *Class and News*, Don Heider, editor. Lanham, Maryland: Rowman & Littlefield, 2004, pp. 87-107.

[43] Jack Lule, 2001, p. 23.

[44] Tim Groeling, Tim and Matthew A. Baum, "Barbarians inside the gates: Partisan news media and the polarization of American political discourse," paper presented to the annual convention of the American Political Science Association, Chicago, Illinois, Aug. 30 –Sept. 2, 2007..

[45] Shanto Iyengar and Kyu S. Hahn, "Red Media, Blue Media: Evidence of Ideological Selectivity in Media Use," *Journal of Communication 59*, 2009, 19-39.

[46] Neda Maghbouleh, "Television," entry in *Class in America: An Encyclopedia*, Robert E. Weir, editor. Westport, Connecticut: Greenwood Press, 2007, pp. 852-856.

[47] Pew Research Center Publications, "The Elusive 90% Solution," March 11, 2011. http://pewresearch.org/pubs/1925/elusive=90-percent-solution-gas-prices. Viewed March 14, 2011.

[48] Edith Efron. *The News Twisters.* Los Angeles, CA: Nash Publishing, 1971.

[49] Robert L. Stevenson, Richard A. Eisinger, Barry M. Feinberg,

Alan B. Kotok, "Untwisting *The News Twisters*: A Replication of Efron's Study," *Journalism Quarterly, 50* (2), June 1973, pp. 211-219.

[50] David Brock. *The Republican Noise Machine.* New York: Crown Publishers, p. 76.

[51] Brock, p. 77.

[52] Brock, pp. 78, 94-100.

[53] Guido Stempel, book reviews, *Journalism Quarterly*, 68 (1-2), 1991, pp. 290-291.

[54] Al Neuharth, "Fewer Newspapers try to dictate votes," USA Today, October 31, 2008, p. 11A; Perspective, "In Ink, It's a Landslide," St. Petersburg Times, November 2, 2008, p. 3; Howard Kurtz, "36 Paper Abandon Bush for Kerry," *Washington Post*, Oct. 27, 2004, p. A13; Greg Mitchell and Joe Strupp, "Bird in the hand for Bush?" *Editor & Publisher, 133* (45), November 6, 2000, pp. 24-27; Dorothy Giobbe, "Dole wins in endorsements," *Editor & Publisher, 129* (43), October 26, 1996, p. 7; George Garneau, "Clinton's the Choice," *Editor & Publisher, 125* (43), Oct. 24, 1992, p. 9; Editorial, "Letting the Sun Shine," *Editor & Publisher, 138* (1) January 1, 2005, p. 19.

[55] Mark D. Harmon, "Papers Endorse Incumbents Four-to-One over Challengers," *Newspaper Research Journal, 28* (3), Summer 2007, pp. 65-75.

[56] Byron St. Dizier, "Editorial Page Editors and Endorsements: Chain-owned v. Independent Newspapers," *Newspaper Research Journal, 8* (1), Winter 1986, pp. 63-68.

[57] Robert W. McChesney, "The Problem of Journalism: a political economic contribution to an explanation of the crisis in contemporary US journalism," *Journalism Studies 4*, 2003, p. 306.

[58] See the Pew Research Center's Project for Excellence in Journalism, The State of the News Media 2012. http://stateofthemedia.org/. Viewed July 23, 2012.

[59] Martin Kaplan, Ken Goldstein, and Matthew Hale, "Local News Coverage of the 2004 Campaign, an Analysis of Nightly Broadcasts in Eleven Markets," The Lear Center Local News Archive, a project of USC Annenberg School and the University of Wisconsin, Feb. 15, 2005. http://www.localnewsarchive.org/. Also see http://bigmedia.org/index.php

[60] Mark D. Harmon, "Bias? Arrogance? Goldberg Liberal Media Claims Fail Logical Test," *Review of Communication, 5* (2-3), April to July 2005, pp. 109-118.

[61] Eric Alterman. *What Liberal Media?* New York: Basic Books, 2003.

[62] Sut Jhally, Noam Chomsky, Edward S. Herman, and Justin Lewis. The Myth of Liberal Media: the propaganda model of news (video). Northampton, MA: Media Education Foundation, 1997.

[63] Michael T. Kaufman, "Reed Irvine, 82, the Founder Of a Media Criticism Group," *The New York Times*, November 19, 2004, p. B9.

[64] Dan Cassino and Peter Woolley, "Some News Leaves People Knowing Less. Part Deux: Many think US is bailing out Greece; NPR, Jon Stewart Out-Fox Cable News," Fairleigh Dickinson University's Public Mind Poll, November 21 and 28, 2011. Retrieved from http://publicmind.fdu.edu. Viewed Nov. 30, 2011.

[65] Steven Kull, principal investigator. *The PIPA/Knowledge Networks Poll. Misperceptions, the Media and the Iraq War.* http://www.pipa.org/OnlineReports/Iraq/IraqMedia_Oct03/IraqMedia_Oct03_pr.pdf. October 2, 2003. Viewed Jan. 24, 2006.

[66] Daniel Kurtzman, "Stephen Colbert at the White House Correspondents' Dinner," About.com, http://www.dailykos.com/story/2006/04/30/206303/-Re-Improved-Colbert-transcript-now-with-complete-text-of-Colbert-Thomas-video. Viewed July 20, 2012.

[67] See Karen Seccombe. *So You Think I Drive a Cadillac?* Boston, MA: Pearson, 2nd ed., 2007.

[68] The poll used for these tables were: Antonis Papacostas, Eurobarometer 67.1: Cultural Values, Poverty and Social Exclusion, Developmental Aid, and Residential Mobility, February-March 2007 [Computer file]. ICPSR21522-v2. Cologne, Germany: GESIS/Ann Arbor, MI: Inter-university Consortium for Political and Social Research [distributors], 2010-06-16. doi:10.3886/ICPSR21522; Bernd Wegener, David Mason, and International Social Justice Project (ISJP). International Social Justice Project, 1991 and 1996 [Computer file]. ICPSR06705-v2. Ann Arbor, MI: Inter-university for Political and Social Research [distributor], 2010-03-04. doi:10.3886/ICPSR06705 ; Bernd Wegener and International Social Justice Project, ISJP (1996-2000). International Social Justice Project, 1996 and 2000 [Computer file]. ICPSR22750-v1. Ann Arbor, MI: Inter-university for Political and Social Research [distributor], 2010-02-08. doi:10.3886/ICPSR22750; Cichomski, Bogdan (principal investigator), Tomasz Jerzynski and Marcin Zielinski. Polish General Social Surveys: machine readable data file and cumulative codebook 1992- 2002. Institute for Social Studies, University of Warsaw, producer and distributor, Warsaw, Poland, 2004; James A. Davis, Tom W. Smith, and Peter V. Marsden. GENERAL SOCIAL SURVEYS, 1972-2008: [Cumulative File, Computer file]. Chicago, IL: National Opinion Research Center [producer], 2009. Storrs, CT: Roper Center for Public Opinion Research, University of Connecticut / Ann Arbor, MI: Inter-university Consortium for Political and Social Research / Berkeley, CA: Computer-assisted Survey Methods Program (http://sda.berkeley.edu), University

of California [distributors], 2009; International Social Survey Program (ISSP). International Social Survey Program: Social Inequality, 1992 [Computer file]. Koeln, Germany: Zentralarchiv fuer Empirische Sozialforschung [producer], 1992. Koeln, Germany: Zentralarchiv fuer Empirische Sozialforschung/Ann Arbor, MI: Inter-university Consortium for Political and Social Research [distributors], 1996.

[69] Mark D. Harmon, "Why People Are Poor/Wealthy: Powerful Frame for Public Attitudes and Opinions," *Baker Center Journal of Applied Public Policy, 4*(1), 73-91.

[70] Mark D. Harmon, "Why People are Poor/Wealthy: Powerful Frames," poster presented to the 7th International Conference on Conceptions of Library and Information Science, London, UK, June 23, 2010; Mark D. Harmon, "Why Poor and Why Rich: Cross-Cultural Consistency in Liberal-Conservative Orientation," research presentation to "Comparing Political Communication Across Time and Space," a conference of the European Communication Research and Education Association's Political Communication Section, Madrid, Spain, October 21, 2011.

[71] Gail Sahar Zucker and Bernard Weiner, "Conservatism and Perceptions of Poverty: An Attributional Analysis," *Journal of Applied Social Psychology, 13*(12), 2006, pp. 925-943.

[72] George Lakoff. *Moral Politics: How Liberals and Conservatives Think.* Chicago: University of Chicago Press, 2002; George Lakoff. *Don't Think of an Elephant: Know Your Values and Frame the Debate.* White River Junction, VT: Chelsea Green Publishing, 2004.

[73] Ronald Inglehart. World Values Survey. European and World Values Surveys four-wave integrated data file, 1981-2004, v.20060423, 2006. Surveys designed and executed by the European Values Study Group and World Values Survey Association. File Producers: ASEP/JDS, Madrid, Spain and Tilburg University,

Tilburg, the Netherlands. File Distributors: ASEP/JDS and GESIS, Cologne, Germany. It is available from the World Values Survey website (http://www.wvsevsdb.com/wvs/WVSData.jsp?Idioma=I) as well as that of the ICPSR and the Association for Religion Data Archives (http://www.thearda.com/Archive/Files/Descriptions/WVSAGG.asp).

[74] Marta Lagos, executive director. Latinobarometer, 2000. [machine-readable data file], Latinobarómetro Corporation [distributor], 2009. Latinobarometer Data Files, http://hdl.handle.net/1902.29/10528.

[75] World Values Survey t=27.127; Latinobarómetro t=9.9057.

Both p <.0001.

[76] Graham F. Wagstaff, "Attitudes to Poverty: The Protestant Ethics, and Political Affiliation: A Preliminary Investigation," *Social Behavior and Personality, 11*(1), 1983, pp. 45-47.

[77] Rajiv Prabhakar, "Wealth Taxes: Stories, Metaphors and Public Attitudes," *The Political Quarterly, 79* (2), April-June 2008, pp 172-178.

[78] Janak Pandey, Yoganand Sinha, Anand Prakash, and R. C. Tripathi, "Right-Left Political Ideologies and Attribution of the Causes of Poverty," *European Journal of Social Psychology, 12* (3), July-September 1982, pp. 327-331.

[79] Maria Nawojczyk and Shane Walton, "Polish Perspectives on the Morality of Capital Accumulation," *Journal of International Studies, 16* (1-2), 2004, pp. 111-132.

[80] Agnieszka Paczynska, "Market Reforms and Democratic Consolidation: the Case of Poland," paper presented to the annual meeting of the American Political Science Association, Boston, Massachusetts, 2002.

[81] John E. Schwarz. *America's Hidden Success.* New York: W. W. Norton & Co., 1988, pp. 49-50.

[82] Molly Ivins, "The Really Dirty Administration: Reagan's," editorial using Justice Department figures, *San Jose Mercury News*, October 23, 1996, p. B6.

[83] Dave Searles Brodhead, "Reagan-Bush-Bush Put Country in Debt," editorial in *The Capital Times* (Madison, Wisconsin), October 17, 2006, p. A7.

[84] John deGraaf, David Wann, and Thomas H. Naylor. *Affluenza: the all consuming epidemic.* San Francisco, CA: Berrett-Koehler, 2001, p. 2.

[85] George Gerbner and Larry Gross, "Living with television: the violence profile," *Journal of Communication, 26* (2), Spring 1976, pp. 173-199; George Gerbner, Larry Gross, Michael F. Eleey, Marilyn Jackson-Beeck, Suzanne Jeffries-Fox, and Nancy Signorelli, "Violence Profile No. 8: The Highlights," *Journal of Communication, 27*, Spring 1977, pp. 171-180; George Gerbner, Larry Gross, Michael F. Eleey, Marilyn Jackson-Beeck, Suzanne Jeffries-Fox, and Nancy Signorelli, "Violence Profile No. 7: Trends in Network Television Drama and Viewer Conceptions of Social Reality, 1967-1975," The Annenberg School of Communications, University of Pennsylvania, April 1976; George Gerbner, Larry Gross, Michael F. Eleey, Marilyn Jackson-Beeck, Suzanne Jeffries-Fox, and Nancy Signorelli, "Cultural Indicators: Violence profile No. 9,' *Journal of Communication, 28*: Summer 1978, pp. 176-207.

[86] Paul M. Hirsch, "The 'scary world' of the nonviewer and other anomalies: a reanalysis of Gerbner et al.'s findings on cultivation analysis. *Communication Research: An International Quarterly 7* (4), October 1980, pp. 403-456. Also see Michael Hughes, "The Fruits of Cultivation Analysis: A Reexamination of Some Effects of Television Viewing," *Public Opinion Quarterly 44* (3), Autumn

1980, pp. 287-302.

87 Juliet B. Schor. *The Overspent American.* New York: Basic Books, 1998, pp. 80-81.

88 Jeffrey A. Kottler. *Exploring and Treating Acquisitive Desire.* Thousand Oaks, CA: Sage, 1999.

89 Alison Grant, "U.S. Workers overworked, overstressed; Long hours threatening our health, family time," Plain Dealer (Cleveland), November 21, 2004; also distributed on Newhouse News Service and Religion News Service, p. A1; Michael Reiss, "Are you suffering from affluenza?" *New Statesman*, August 5, 2002.

90 James J. Farrell. *One Nation Under Goods: Malls and the Seductions of American Shopping.* Washington, DC: Smithsonian Books, 2003.

91 John de Graff and Vivia Boe, producers; Scott Simon, host. *Affluenza* [videorecording, VHS, 56 min.], Olney, PA, Bullfrog Films, 1997; Vivia Boe and John de Graff, producers; W. Urbanska, host. *Escape from Affluenza: Simple living and its rewards* [videorecording, DVD, 56 minutes], Seattle, WA, KCTS, 2008.

92 M. Joseph Sirgy, Dong-Jin Lee, Rustan Kosenko, H. Lee Meadow, Don Rahtz, Muris Cicic, Guang Xi Jin, Duygun Yarsuvat, David L. Blenkhorn, and Newell Wright, "Does Television Viewership Play a Role in the Perception of Quality of Life?" *Journal of Advertising, 27* (1), 1998, pp. 125-142.

93 Moniek Buijzen and Patti M. Valkenburg, "The Impact of Television Advertising on Children's Christmas Wishes," *Journal of Broadcasting and Electronic Media, 44* (3), 2000, pp. 456-470.

94 Moniek Buijzen and Patti M. Valkenburg, "The Unintended

Effects of Television Advertising: A Parent-Child Survey," *Communication Research 30* (5), October 2003, pp. 483-503.

[95] Tim Kasser. *The High Price of Materialism.* Cambridge, Massachusetts: MIT Press, 2002, pp. 18-21.

[96] Mark D. Harmon, "Affluenza: Television Use and Cultivation of Materialism," *Mass Communication & Society 4* (4), November 2001, pp. 405-418.

[97] Mark D. Harmon, "Affluenza: A World Values Test," *Gazette, 68* (2), April 2006, pp. 119-130.

[98] Newell D. Wright and Val Larsen, "Materialism and Life Satisfaction: a Meta-Analysis," *Journal of Consumer Satisfaction, Dissatisfaction and Complaining Behavior 6*, 1993, pp. 158-165.

[99] James A. Davis, Tom W. Smith, and Peter V. Marsden. General Social Surveys, 1972-2004. [Cumulative File, Computer file]. 2nd ICPSR version. Chicago, IL: National Opinion Research Center [producer], 2005. Storrs, CT: Roper Center for Public Opinion Research, University of Connecticut / Ann Arbor, MI: Inter-university Consortium for Political and Social Research / Berkeley, CA: Computer-assisted Survey Methods Program (http://sda.berkeley.edu), University of California [distributors], 2005.

[100] William A. Gamson, David Croteau, William Hoynes, and Theodore Sasson, "Media Images and the Social Construction of Reality," *Annual Review of Sociology, 18*, 1992, pp. 373-393.

[101] Thorstein Veblen. *The Theory of the Leisure Class: An Economic Study in the Evaluation of Institutions.* New York: MacMillan, 1899.

[102] Vance Packard. *The Status Seekers.* New York: McKay, 1959; John Kenneth Galbraith. *The Affluent Society.* Boston, MA:

Houghton Mifflin, 1958.

[103] Arnold L. Farr. *Critical Theory and Democratic Vision: Herbert Marcuse and Recent Liberation Philosophies.* New York: Lexington Books, 2009.

[104] Richard Heeks, "Emerging Markets: Information Technology and Gross National Happiness," *Communications of the ACM* (Association of Computing Machinery) 55 (4), April 2012, pp. 24-26.

[105] Daron Acemoglu and James A. Robinson. *Why Nations Fail: The Origins of Power, Prosperity, and Poverty.* New York: Crown Business, 2012.

[106] George G. Kirstein, "The Day the Ads Stopped," *The Nation*, June 1, 1964, pp. 555-557.

[107] John C. Stauber and Sheldon Rampton. *Toxic Sludge is Good for You: Lies, Damn Lies, and the Public Relations Industry.* Monroe, ME: Common Courage Press, 1995; Margo Robb; John C Stauber; Mark Crispin Miller; Stuart Ewen; Amy Goodman 1957. *Toxic sludge is good for you: the public relations industry unspun* [video]. Northampton, MA: Media Education Foundation, 2002.

[108] http://youtu.be/ZRuf9gdEgfw. Viewed July 18, 2012.